FROM BULLS TO BALLS

From one "Geoffrey"
to another

D1421862

FROM BULLS TO BALLS

Geoffrey Leet

ARTHUR H. STOCKWELL LTD.
Elms Court   Ilfracombe   Devon
Established 1898

© *Geoffrey Leet, 1997*
First published in Great Britain, 1997
All rights reserved.
No part of this publication may be reproduced
or transmitted in any form or by any means,
electronic or mechanical, including photocopy,
recording, or any information storage and
retrieval system, without permission
in writing from the copyright holder.

British Library Cataloguing-in-Publication Data.
A catalogue record for this book is available
from the British Library.

ISBN 0 7223 3088-X

Printed in Great Britain by
Arthur H. Stockwell Ltd.
Elms Court   Ilfracombe
Devon

The Winchester .32 barked and the rush of the bull was stopped. Unfortunately my horse on which I was astride, what with the bark of the rifle and the rush of the bull, found all this was a bit much and took off at a frantic gallop.

More by luck than any horsy judgement I was able to stay in the saddle, fiddle with the safety catch of the Winchester, stick it back into its leather long holster, which was situated just in front of my booted and spurred right leg and rein in my galloping steed.

I should perhaps explain that I was a Jackeroo. What the devil is a Jackeroo? Well it was, and probably still is, an Australian cowboy. As against my American counterpart I was very seldom armed, but this particular day was unique in that four of us had been sent out to find four bulls and shoot them *dead*.

Why? Because the bulls were deformed and were responsible for breeding hundreds of deformed sons and daughters and this had to stop *now*.

The *little* place I was on was a cattle station of some 4,000 square miles, situated about 1,000 miles due west of Brisbane, east of Alice but not all that much in Australian distance, and it contained very roughly about 40,000 head of cattle.

The bulls concerned were deformed in the hind quarters — in fact you could say that their back legs were almost entwined. How that happened the Lord only knows, but a lot of very odd things happen out in the wilds of Australia, and this was one of them. It wouldn't have been so bad if they weren't so fertile, for more or less every cow they served produced a nice little calf *but* their hind legs were next to useless.

I was just 18 when I went out to Australia. I left my Public School at 17, served a ghastly year in the City of London, and whilst my parents were taking a trip to India on business, I left them a note and departed with a letter of introduction to a company in Brisbane who just might give me a job.

Arriving in Brisbane I found that the man I should have met, had died in a traffic accident the week before. I went the rounds of all the headquarters of cattle stations in Brisbane with no luck till I came to one who asked the usual questions as to whether I could ride a horse, but then as an afterthought, asked whether I could tap out Morse.

"Morse?" I asked. "How many words a minute do you want?" To which he replied that he hadn't a clue *but* if I could tap out Morse, I had myself a job.

I thanked him and departed to catch a train out west, my fare being paid for by the Company. I kept wondering how many words I could remember of Morse, and why on earth on a cattle station they wanted someone who could receive and send Morse.

I spent some three days on that train and was met by three horsemen leading a fourth horse and was invited to, "Get my arse aloft," or words to that effect.

We rode all that very hot day with not a lot of conversation, but one of my future mates asked what riding experience I had had to which I answered quickly that I really knew nothing about horses and hoped that they would teach me. This went down well for I had been warned about this sort of thing. *Never*, as a Bastard Pom (their everyday expression for an Englishman) say that you can do *anything*, for they will at once think that you are saying that you can do things better than they can.

So as we rode into the sunset, they were more than kind and showed me things one could do with a horse that on the hunting fields of England, one would never have dreamt of doing.

We came to a water-hole with a few trees around it, tethered one horse to a branch, hobbled the others and turned them loose, started a fire, boiled up a billy-can and I had my first bush meal. I was given a swag, which really is a sort of waterproof sleeping bag, and told to get me head down, which I was more than glad to do, for my bottom felt raw, my neck ached and I was dead beat.

I was woken at about 04.00 hrs. and told to ride the tethered horse out and find the others, one of which had a bell attached round his neck. I was also told that this task was *always* done riding without a saddle as the noise of the creaking leather might frighten the hobbled horses.

Although I had done a bit of riding in England I had never ridden a horse without a saddle before, let alone in the dark, so I bridled him up and somewhat gingerly hoisted myself onto his back. My confidence grew as he seemed to have no intention of casting me off onto the cold sand of the semi-desert and off we set, listening for a bell. I carried with me some halters for the three that I had to find and bring back to the camp, and I soon found my three, all peacefully grazing.

So far so good, but I had first to catch one, shove a halter round him, get him quiet so that I could bend down and untie the hobbles, all the while holding my nag *and* repeat this exercise with the other three. Anyway, after a while I achieved what seemed at the time an impossible task and rode back surrounded by horses, to be met with some astonishment by the other men who by this time were up and the billy was boiling away. I learnt afterwards that the exercise I had been on was to test me to see whether I was a useless drag on them and the cattle station as a whole, which I presume meant that I would have been sent back to Brisbane.

And so we cleared up after a hasty breakfast, which to my surprise consisted mainly of dried beef. I'd never had dried beef before, let alone for breakfast, but never said a word, but chewed on.

We rode for most of that morning and just as the sun was really starting to get unpleasantly hot, we arrived at the cattle station, situated on the side of a large expanse of water, with the manager's house to the side of various outbuildings.

We were greeted with some curiosity by the rest of the cowhands, for most of them had never set eyes on an Englishman before and wondered whether, as a race, they looked the same as anybody else.

There were five whites in all and a couple of black boys, who, for some reason or other were quite ignored, and I made up the sixth member of the camp which seemed quite a small work-force to look after some 40,000 head on 4,000 square miles.

Bill the head stockman was a kindly soul, although somewhat taciturn to start off with, after finding out that I knew next to nothing about horses. He was aged somewhere in his fifties but it was hard to tell, for everyone was tanned brown. They were all lean and very fit and after expressing, not all that silently, what they thought of the

3

Pommy accent, we got on quite well. I heard afterwards that the stockmen who had come down to bring me back from the rail head were not a little surprised that I hadn't fallen off on the way.

Charlie was the camp cook, no more than about 5' tall, and he used to cook up some very good meals out in the bush. His provisions were carried on two pack ponies, and he taught me how to build a fire without using a match, which was more than handy.

Frank was the tallest of the lot — a good 6'4", aged about 40 and had done ten years in jail for killing a man in a fight in Sydney. I only learnt this interesting fact after some six months sleeping next to him when we were away from the station and out in the bush. He used to keep on asking questions about London and how big was it, and this went on till I went off to sleep.

Syd was the youngest and took an instant dislike to me, even before I opened my Pommy mouth, I could feel him glaring at me and it was he who would lead me into my first serious fight.

Most days we saddled-up after breakfast and rode off on some job or other and for days I could not understand why my horse, usually a placid female would, as soon as I had got my bottom onto the saddle, buck me off.

One day, on examining my saddle-cloth, I found the remnants of a prickly burr on the underside so that when I put my weight on it, it pressed into my mare's back which must have been somewhat painful — thus the bucking.

I knew that when I had hung the cloth up at night it was clean, so someone was doing this and so I watched the next day whilst we were having breakfast. Syd made some remark and left the camp fire, and without being too obvious I watched his every movement and sure enough, it only took him a second or two to loose the surcingle, slide a hand up under the cloth and come back to the fire.

So I thought that two could play at this game and the opportunity came. Syd went off somewhere and I had a moment to switch burrs. I took mine out and shoved it under his cloth and then waited to see the fun, and sure enough Syd hit the desert sand as soon as he was mounted.

The trouble was that when *I* fell off I generally landed on my backside and was quite winded for a moment or two. Syd on the other hand landed like a cat, and looking up saw me laughing my silly head off. In a flash he knew what had happened and here was his chance to beat this Bastard Pommy into a pulp and he came at me with a rush.

What little fighting I had done was never serious, and nine times out of ten took place in a boxing ring at school with large gloves. One was taught that the correct thing to do was to face your opponent, with your left foot forward and your left hand ready to thrust into the face in front of you.

I soon found out that this bit of so-called information was not universally known. Syd had never heard of it for the next thing I knew was that one of his heavy elastic sided boots came thudding into my lower stomach, obviously aimed at my balls. It took the wind right out of my sails and I stumbled forward, clutching my tum.

For a fleeting moment luck took charge and my bowed head butted the rushing Syd in that nice little cavity just below the breastbone and he, like me, was falling breathless onto the sand. At that moment I remembered our ex Sgt. Major at school, yelling, "use an uppercut," which I was able to do, and caught Syd on the side of the jaw as he sank in front of me. Much to my surprise this blow laid young Syd out flat, someone handed me a wet towel, and I found myself hovering beside Syd wiping his face and muttering my apologies.

Syd came round and peace was restored and in fact Syd called me 'Mate' which was a great step forward from being spoken to as that 'Bastard Pom'.

Lastly there was Mac. I never learned his proper name, but he had come from Scotland years ago and had never lost his accent. He had been a small farmer somewhere just North of Glasgow. The farm was only a few acres and the whole family tried to make a living off it which Mac found frustrating to a degree and he had come out to Australia with the idea of saving money and buying a spread.

Out in the bush I gradually learned things that one should *never* do, such as never step over a log facing the sun for snakes would lie up in the sun and if you trod on one, and were bitten, your chances of survival were slim. A ton sized bullock would, if bitten, always head for the nearest water-hole and if the water was more than a thousand yards he wouldn't make it. On the subject of snakes, in your kit, you always carried a razor blade and some blue crystals. Should you be bitten and on your own, you would have to grit your teeth, make a cross cut over the two teeth marks of the snake, suck and spit if you were able, and then pour in the blue crystals, bind the wound up and keep your fingers crossed.

The other little bit of advice was to do with the loo. At rare times we would all return to the Station and of course use the loo instead of making a hole in the sand, doing the necessary and covering it up. I was told *never* use the loo without lifting up the lid and having a look for scorpions who had a habit of biting your balls.

I still have the habit, much to amusement of my wife and children.

It was on my third or fourth day at the Station when the Station Manager came up to me and said that he wanted to send a message by radio to Brisbane and would I come along and send it.

I soon found out that their so-called radio sending equipment was a trifle different to whàt I had been used to. Firstly the electricity was generated by the operator, in this case me, on a treadle. The faster I pedalled the further I could send my signal. Our call sign was Victor Kilo and some numbers which I have now forgotten and the other difference was my sending key. Previously I had used an up and down key but this one was sideways, which took a bit of getting used to.

Anyway I pedalled away, giving my call sign and asking if Brisbane was receiving me and after some while, when I was sweating away, Brisbane finally came on the air and I was able, very slowly to pass the signal across some 1,000 miles.

Soon came the first of four musters. This meant that we tried to collect together some 10,000 head of cattle into an area of some five miles and in the middle of this, generally near some convenient water-hole, we set up a mustering camp.

Then the real work started because every calf or unbranded beast had to be caught, dehorned, and if a bull calf, castrated and, of course, branded with the station brand.

A large fire was started and branding irons rested in the flames. A bunch of about 200 animals were rounded up and we then set about the task of separating the unbranded calves from the rest. This was all done on horseback, the idea being to sling a lariat around the neck of the calf concerned and at the same time, bringing your own steed to an abrupt halt, always assuming that you have not missed the calf, then two men would 'throw' the animal.

By 'throw' I don't mean the animal was picked up and flung somewhere. Oh no, and this was where one started to learn just a little bit about working *with* and possibly *on* animals, for what happened was this. Imagine the beast concerned, with a taught lariat round its protesting neck, was connected to the horse where the lariat came from. One man would come in front of the animal and hold its nostrils, whilst another would grasp its tail and at a given signal, both men would tug left and the animal would fall on its right side. The man at the rear end grasped the right leg of the animal and put his left leg behind the hock of the animal.

The beast couldn't move, and all this, from the throwing part, took about 30 seconds. Then the 'brander' darted forward and placed his red hot iron on the thigh of the animal and held it there for a few seconds and his job was done. Another man came forward and lopped off both horns and applied hot tar to the bleeding holes. If the animal was a bull calf he was castrated — again a job which took all of 45 seconds. Lastly a tattoo brand was placed in the ear of the animal, the lariat released and the calf wandered off to find his mother.

A good team could get through about 50 animals every hour till the heat of the midday sun became a bit much and everyone took a break in the cool of a tree and had some tucker, prepared by Charlie. Without fail this was steak, spuds and very rarely some greens out of a tin, plus some 'damper' which was bread made without proper yeast, although Charlie did at times produce yeast made from potatoes, which made a change.

Charlie's spud yeast had the alarming habit of exploding in the bottle. As it was carried amongst a host of other cooking items on one of the pack ponies this poor animal would then take off at a fast pace, throwing pots and pans all over the place pursued by an irate Charley.

During my midday break, I used to strip off and go for a swim in the water-hole. My mates thought I was nuts and would catch my death of cold, and I cannot remember ever seeing any of them wash their bodies or anything bar for a sock or two.

I would send out a message to other stations on our boundaries with my sweating treadle Morse radio, and they would send in teams of stockmen to see whether we had any of their branded cattle and if so take them back to their own part of the country.

Mustering would go on week after week till all the cattle we could find had been treated, and at each muster we would find some calves with twisted hind legs, and on one muster we actually rounded up a bull with the same fault, and he we shot forthwith.

Sometime after all the mustering was over the manager decided we ought to go out and see whether we could find any more of these bulls. If they were allowed to go on breeding, in time the whole herd would become useless.

I was one of the stockmen sent out to see what we could find.

We were shown a photo of the tracks these animals made, which was quite distinctive, for the track of one leg dragged across the track of another. Each of us drew a Winchester from the store, plus a few rounds, loaded up a pack pony with food and water and off we went. We each had a compass and was told to aim in a direction some 5 degrees off west, so one of us, which was me, was heading due west. I had Frank and Syd on my left and Mac was on my right.

What a lonely place the Bush is with not a soul in sight and only the odd kangaroo or wallaby loping along — otherwise nothing — flatness all round. I looked at my compass from time to time and made myself a mark on the horizon for the three of us, my mare Shirley, my pack pony, who I called George and me to aim for.

I came to a small water-hole that evening and decided I would make camp. There was a bit of grass around, so I hobbled both horses, made myself a fire and put the billy on to boil. I remembered that to take the billy off the fire, I needed two sticks. When the water has boiled and the tea put in, one inserts the two sticks into the handle of the billy and by pressing the sticks together it can be taken off the fire without the hands being burnt.

I Rolled out my swag and as the sun went down climbed into it with my rifle for company and was asleep within minutes.

I Woke with a start. It was still dark and I felt I was being moved, and could hear heavy breathing. Opening one cautious eye I found Shirley, indicating that she knew I had brought some oats along and could she have a nibble.

All my life I have felt quite at home with animals mainly, I think, because years ago, an uncle of mine who farmed taught me a simple little ploy. This involved having a pee near an animal and should he or she cover it with their own, they at once, due to some odd animal lore, felt you were a sort of blood brother. I had done this with Shirley when I was first given her and she at once did her stuff — my mates thought I was nuts.

Anyway, I fed the girl, caught George and fed him and then lit my fire, brewed up, ate some damper and off we set just as the dawn was starting to break. In an hour's time we crossed a lot of cattle tracks and there as plain as could be was the track of an animal dragging a leg. We altered course a bit and started to follow and quite soon caught up with the tail end of the herd.

I found a bit of feed for George and turned him loose as I could not start cutting out a bull with George attached to me with a line.

Nudging Shirley to a slow canter I went through this mob with an eye out for the bull and finally found him. He was not inclined to play ball with a lone horseman for he turned and charged and I also turned and ran till he got fed up with an unequal race. He returned to his wives, about fifty all told counting the odd calf, and led them into an area of bush.

I circled the bush but nothing appeared and I was wondering what next to do for I was not inclined to wend my way home admitting that I had found a bull and done nothing about it, so I shouted. It didn't matter a hoot what I shouted but I had the feeling that the bull would not care for this sort of semi taunting. I was right, for there was a crashing of bushes and out he came, paused to view where the enemy was and *charged.*

Now me and a rifle are quite happy together if we are lying down and I am allowed to get the foresight lined up with the back sight *and* the target — but this was different. I had never shot anything from the back of a horse, and Shirley, bless her one white sock, took a dim view of the whole set-up and was fidgeting, which didn't help my aiming ability.

I aimed somewhat hastily, remembering to squeeze the trigger and not tug it, and the Winchester thundered its salute across the silent bush and the equally silent .32 bullet sped on its way and hit the bull — now only some thirty yards away — in the shoulder and down he went. By this time, Shirley had had quite enough and was on her way to safer pastures.

It took me at least half a mile to reassure Shirley that I really did *not* want to continue in the direction she had started but wanted to return and put that poor bull out of its agony. Snorting with not so silent nerves she allowed me to guide her back and there was the bull still on the ground, unable to rise, and I was able to put the second round through his brain and that was that — or nearly so. In the cattle camp we were allowed to kill one steer a week if we were out working and my mates liked either the sirloin or any other part of the animal concerned but they all thought the filet was junk. I used to cut out the filet, which only lasted a couple of days in that heat, but as meat went, I had my fill.

As the poor beast was dead I thought, why not, there would be fifty dingoes round the carcass within a few hours, so I cut him up and removed enough filet to make my evening meal. I returned the next day to the Station and having cut off the station brand, I presented this to the manager, who remarked kindly that Pommies did at times have their uses.

Three bulls had been found and shot, which left one roaming away somewhere, but I was destined to have a stint at boundary riding. I was always a bit of a twit when someone asked, "Any volunteers," and in this case the manager wanted someone to ride the eastern boundary.

Sounds easy really, just following a fence which had two barbed and one plain wire till it ended, repairing any breaks in the wire and then returning. But this job generally lasted a whole fortnight — a week out and a week back, *alone* — just Shirley, George the pack-horse and me.

When I first arrived at the cattle station I was wandering round the homestead when I came upon a man sleeping on a veranda. His

Stetson was pulled over his eyes and in the Stetson were two holes — two in the front of the hat and two at the rear. Having fiddled about with rifles when in the school OTC, I thought that they must be bullet holes. They *looked* like bullet holes and with little thought I leaned over and woke the sleeping figure. Without a great degree of apology I asked him what the holes were in his Stetson. A strong brown arm came up, lifted the hat just a fraction, viewed my leaning body and uttered just four words which were quite succinct in that they spelt out, "Fuck off, Pommy Bastard," so I did just that and forgot the whole scene.

Normally in my day wages were the large sum of 17s.6d. per week and 'all found', which meant that you were fed and watered, given a riding horse, a pack pony and a saddle and bridle. If you wanted a spare horse you broke one in yourself and for every 'break' you were presented with the large sum of £5, which sounds a piece of cake, but there were snags. Firstly there were *no* horses kept in a small paddock *but* there were *brumbies* that you could catch. A brumbie is a wild horse, and I mean just that. For a start it has probably never seen a man and you have to catch it by slinging a lariat round its neck and grinding it to a halt.

Actually that isn't quite right for when several of us wanted a spare pony, we organized a drive and mustered thirty or more brumbies into a fenced in area where, with a bit of luck, we would catch the horse we fancied.

To earn our fiver we had to saddle and bridle the animal, ride out a few hundred yards and bring it back. It was then made to stand still — a quite impossible task unless we followed the well tried practice done in cattle camp which went like this. Firstly the animal was persuaded into a 'crush', which is a narrow passage with a gate at either end into which a horse or cow will only just fit and has no room to lash out. We then placed a saddle blanket underneath a heavy pack saddle on the back of the animal, tightened the lot with a surcingle, put on a head collar which was attached to a very long leading rein and opened the gate into quite a small coral.

The horse takes off but cannot go far, firstly because of the wooden railings and secondly its head is held on the end of the long rein. It is then persuaded it to go round and round this small area and if it stops, a stock whip is cracked behind its tail. There came a time when the poor beast was somewhat tired, and so for that matter were we, but more was to come. Back into the crush we sent the horse, took off the pack saddle and placed a riding saddle in its place, but still retained the long leading rein which was held by a mate. We then showed it that a man was aloft, and not a pack saddle and continued to go round and round.

We then turned it out into a small paddock and repeated the same exercise over the course of the next three days and then came the time when, instead of having a halter, a proper bridle and bit was put on. The animal was taught to respond to the rein being pulled either to the left or right and to respond accordingly and when both were pulled it meant stop. During these three days I used to be tossed off at least once every fifteen minutes but the other men, of course, fared a lot better.

Then came the final test where we saddled-up, without the crush this time, took a deep breath and shouted for the gate to come down. The head stockman would be watching and then it was up to you to take your horse out and bring him back without too much trouble. If you did that you got your fiver.

In the slack season after all the mustering had been done there was another way of earning quite a lot of money on a cattle station and this was to do with the Indian Army.

The Indian Army wanted horses, hundreds of them, but of course delivered to India by ship and Bombay was the port.

The Army would get in touch with our company down in Brisbane and ask if they could supply, say 100 broken to saddle horses.

Sometimes the Army would send out one of their officers to a cattle station to view what was on offer. They never came to us *but* they wanted horses and so several of us banded together, firstly to round up a herd of brumbies, say about 100, out of which we culled at least 50 and settled down to the not so gentle job of breaking them in to the head stockman's satisfaction.

Instead of the somewhat lowly figure of £5 for what one might call a 'Home break' we got £30 per head, delivered to the railhead which was at least 200 miles due east of us.

I was included in this threesome because I was the only one who knew Morse and all the signals came to me and I would tell the manager what was wanted by head office. In fact I was quite important, one way and another, (or thought I was). I was the link over nearly a thousand miles and by this time my Morse had improved quite a bit.

Our first fifty reluctant Indian Army mounts finally were broken in to the satisfaction of the head stockman, but then the Army signalled through that 50 was not enough and they wanted another 50, so the three of us rode off searching for Brumbies.

It might sound an easy job, but there were snags. You did not want a mare with foal at foot, you did not also want a pregnant mare and you did not want an old stallion, for they were, in the main, impossible to bring to a saddle and bridle.

So one searched, sometimes a hundred miles or so, but even when you had found what you wanted, you always had the job of keeping the mob to heel so to speak, for a horse, especially the wild ones had a turn of speed which at times was unmatchable.

But in the end, after about a week we rode into the station homestead with a little over 50 not so willing horses and settled down to the task of breaking them into saddle and bridle.

Then there was the job of finding when a train would be available to truck our hundred horses down to Brisbane. Once again I hammered away at my Morse key and finally all was ready and the three of us started on our two hundred mile trek down to the rail head.

Now when you are doing the same job with cattle the rule is round about 10–20 miles per day as otherwise you take all the fat off the animal, but with horses, especially semi-wild ones, some days were in the region of double that and the nights were hell.

Two of us riding herd on this lot all through the long night whilst the lucky one curled up in his swag.

We lost about a dozen on the way, how they escaped I just don't know, but the count at the rail head did not tally with the one with which we set out.

Part of this 'horsey' bargain was that one of us would go with the horses down to Brisbane and deliver the animals to the ship and what was more take the journey by sea to Bombay and deliver our not so quiet steeds over to the Army.

So we tossed up for the fun of going on this trip and Bill and I lost and John carried on with his horses and I heard long afterwards the antics at the docks of Bombay when horses were hoisted over the side in a sling and let down gently on the dockside for the Army to take over. For then the fun started. These horses that we had broken in months ago and never had a man on their backs for all that time took a gloomy view of what was in store for them and riders were flung off left right and centre and two were thrown into the dock itself.

But in the end the Army won, as they always do, and our horses trotted away to their future, very much divorced from the life that they had known on the desert plains of central Australia.

Bill and I rode back to the station and he got me talking about England and schools and life in general, rowing at Henley, girl friends, and he wondered why on earth I had come all this way to lead this sort of life. I replied that I wanted to see how other people lived and this was a way of doing it and enjoying it at the same time.

Well, said Bill, you have certainly learnt to ride *almost* as well as us — and that remark I treasure to this day.

BROKEN BONES

If one is stupid enough to break a bone, then make certain you do it near to a doctor or a hospital but *never* out in the Australian bush with the only mode of transport — a horse, and *no* doctor available.

We were on our usual quarterly muster, which was quite hard work, especially with the temperature hovering around 120 degrees in the *shade*.

Each day we would ride steadily west, gathering up stray herds of cattle till we had collected about 500 head. Then a day or maybe two was spent separating the unwilling calves from their mothers. This was done mainly on horseback. We would ride through the mob, spot a 'customer' and work him away from his mother to the outside of the mob and then came the tricky business of slinging a lariat round its neck and stopping Shirley, my faithful mare in her tracks. With a bit of luck this would throw the 'customer' onto the ground, where two cowhands would do the usual business of branding and de-horning.

Shirley, my mare had become a dab hand at this business. I only had to show her a 'customer' and she would edge it to the waiting cowhands, dodging this way and that, sometimes on just two legs, without a thought of me perched somewhat precariously in my saddle. But she and I were real mates and she was really fond of me, mainly I think because quite by accident she had smelt my urine. One day I wanted a pee and had stopped her, dismounted, spent my penny, whilst holding her reins, and surprise surprise, she 'nosed' *it* and moved forward and did her stuff on top of mine. I think this meant that we were friends for life.

And so we proceeded westward and at our furthest point trouble struck. I had been trying with no great success to extract a large calf from the mob and suddenly it made a dash into quite thick scrub and the head stockman yelled at me to go after the 'bastard' which Shirley and I did. But there were small trees here and there and Shirley, bless her one white sock took one tree just a wee bit too close for the comfort of my nearside ankle and we hit it with a bang. My leg was knocked out of the leather stirrup cup and I felt a desperate pain in my ankle, so leaving one leg dangling, I reined Shirley in and forgot that wretched calf, all I wanted to do was to get back to the camp because I felt faint and looking down at my ankle, it looked to be stuck out at an odd angle.

I came back and the head stockman asked somewhat briskly what I had done with the calf, so told him what had happened and he sent another cowhand off to bring the animal back.

"Can you walk?" asked he.

"I think I have broken a bone in my ankle," I replied.

"Bloody hell, do you remember that we are at least five days away from the station?"

I said that the point had crossed my mind. So he called a couple of hands and they gently lifted me off Shirley's backside and after trying to put just a little weight on this twisted limb and they saw that the pain was excruciating, they all took my weight and laid me down on a blanket.

Jim, the head stockman then tried to get my elastic sided riding boot off but the pain was frantic, so out came his sheath knife and before I could say a word, he had cut my beautiful boot in two and then we all saw the damage.

"Bloody hell." Jim was a man of few words, and what he then said, put the fear of God into my young frame. "Sorry chum but we have to straighten this thing back to normal and it's going to hurt, otherwise by the time we get back, it might set in this odd shape. Hold the lad down you lot."

And then thankfully, and by good fortune, I fainted, and came to to find my leg and ankle straightened, hurting like hell. It was held in a splint and in one of the wooden boxes that we used to hold tucker. One end had been taken out and there was my poor limb in a sort of open ended coffin, with mud from the nearby water-hole all round it. A sort of natural plaster.

By this time it was time for the evening meal and they were all most kind to the boy who used to be called 'that Pommy Bastard' but now had been elevated to 'mate'. They brought the food to me, they levered me into my swag and then I remembered that I *must* have an evening pee before I turned in. This had some amusing moments because of course I couldn't walk, so two of them carried me between them till they thought we were far enough away from the camp, set me down on the good leg, asked whether I wanted any further help. "Just a little balance would be handy," I replied, so that was how that was done. So back to my swag I was lifted and after a while, the ankle calmed down and I went off to sleep.

The morning came as all mornings do, bright sun as is usual in the desert, we cooked and ate our breakfast and there were deep discussions as to how I was going to make the next five days or so. I could not walk, so that was out and nobody knew if I could ride, for there was this open box like affair with my leg well and truly plastered into it and hanging down without any hope of getting it into a stirrup.

Luckily Shirley was quiet, she seldom skitted about, she was placid to a degree and that helped and so I was lifted aloft, the injured leg left dangling in its wooden 'coffin' and the other foot safely in its stirrup which we lengthened somewhat so that I could lean over slightly and try and balance my somewhat peculiar body weight.

And so with many anxious looks from the others, off we set at a slow walk, and so far everything was quite reasonable and in fact we even raised a slow canter and still I was able to stay aloft.

Trouble came after we had gone for about a couple of hours and I wanted to spend a penny and I must admit looking back, the next five minutes or so were hilarious to a degree. You see in the normal turn of events, if when you are riding along, and you want to attend to the needs of nature, you rein in your horse, take your feet out of their 'irons' and down you get onto the ground.

As I could not dismount I asked the nearest couple to give me a hand, to which they replied that it might be easier for all concerned if I was going to make a habit of this, that I stay where I was and pee off the back of the horse.

I thought about this for a fleeting moment and it sounded sense, so I undid my flys, pulled out my manhood and waited ... and waited ... and *nothing* happened. I wanted to have a pee but it was impossible.

"I can't do it," I said.

Don't be a stupid Pom, said one, go on have another try. To which I replied that *if* he wanted to have a pee, then he try off the back of *his* horse.

And he did just that, or to be more exact, he also tried and he couldn't either, and then they all got interested in this performance and here were six hard bitten men, all with their manhood in respective hands and good old ripe Australianese was being bellowed out over the desert.

Nobody could do this simple exercise whilst mounted on a horse, so two of them lifted me off, muttering their disbelief.

Day five came much to my relief and when we arrived at the homestead I was lifted into the room where the Morse instrument was situated and I sent a signal down to base saying what had happened. By this time the mud from the water hole had set well and truly and when the flying doctor appeared he had to break open the cast round my leg to examine the limb.

17

After I had been able to put a little weight on it the doctor said there was nothing that he could do, it had set reasonably well and he praised the efforts of the head stockman and his mates and said that I had been more than fortunate *but* when I got back near a hospital, I should have it X-rayed to make certain that all was well.

I volunteered to do boundary riding because we were paid the princely sum of £5 per week, and again all found.

So one morning off I set on Shirley with George laden with spare wire and tucker trailing behind on his usual long rope following this endless fence. Where it was broken, I dismounted, tied up both horses and set to and mended the break, which generally was caused by kangaroos trying to get over the fence. Where it was slack, I tightened it up and only very rarely would a broken fence post be found and I replaced it by digging in a new one, which George carried. If I ran out of posts I had to get the axe out and make one from the growing timber. Hot work in that heat.

At night I made camp as per usual, cooked some food and crept into my swag with my rifle nestling against my thigh, and my two horses hobbled and munching away at the sparse grass that grew all round.

I remember the second day I shot a bush turkey which made a nice change from the everlasting dried beef, and it was on the fourth day out that I found myself actually talking to myself *and* giving an answer. I was, to put it mildly, bored stiff.

That evening to while away the time, I set a tin on one of the fence posts and settled down to do some target practice — I had plenty of ammunition — but when I came to the end of the fence and very thankfully turned for home, some three days off the camp, I ran out of bloody tins. I had shot them all to bits, because I was so tired of doing nothing and now, with only a rifle to relieve the boredom, I was frustrated to a degree. But that very evening, without thinking, I took off my Stetson in the cool air, cocked the Winchester, threw the hat high into the air and fired at it and — *missed*.

But I was happy. I had something to do, and if there was one thing I would do before reaching the homestead, it was to hit that dammed hat.

18

I hit it on the last night and arrived back as happy as a sand boy, washed down my two faithful friends and turned them out into a paddock and went to sit on the veranda but soon sleep came and I remember tilting my hat over my eyes before I nodded off. I was woken by a not so gentle foot on my backside and a voice saying, "Well, you made it. What, only one bleeding hole. Good on yer mate." It was the man I had met in that very same spot months ago when *he* had just returned from *his* stint of boundary riding. No more pommy bastard, I was a *mate*. I had arrived. I looked at my Stetson with some wonder and felt ten foot tall.

I had by this time earned some time off and departed by various means, such as horse, wagon, and truck down to Sydney where I had some cousins, but found when I got there that they were on holiday, so booked myself into a small hotel instead for ten days.

Nice place. Clean and tidy; but when I first went in, there was a female behind the desk who wanted to know when I wanted to leave. Odd sort of question I thought, but maybe that's the way they do things down under, so reckoning that it would take me three whole days to get back to the station, I told her when I wanted to leave and she then asked me for my money there and then.

She saw the look of astonishment on my youthful face and explained that was the way that they did things in this hotel and it saved me from being mugged and my money stolen, which when you look at it, had some sense to it.

So I handed over my hard earned money and was shown to my room. Nice room; the only thing odd about it was that it had a double bed, but I thought no more of it and went downstairs to the bar. I asked for a beer and another chap, hearing my Pommy accent came over and made his number, so to speak and asked which one I fancied.

I thought he meant the beer and started off by telling him where I had come from and this was the beer that I was used to in Australia.

"I don't mean the beer, I mean the *Sheilas*" said he, as if explaining something to a backward child. And then I looked around the bar area and there were a lot of girls, mostly on their own and I remembered when I first came into this 'hotel' there were quite a few lone females doing nothing in particular.

"Do you mean to say that this place is a....", and I hesitated at the very thought that this innocent (or reasonably so) Pommy was really in a *brothel.*

"That's right, mate, that's what it is and most of the smaller hotels are all the same. Perfectly safe and as clean as clean, so take your pick. Book her in with Mother and it comes out of the 'swag' you gave her when you first booked in."

And he was right, this new friend of mine. As a matter of interest, a year later he and I went panning for gold together up north of Brisbane, where the form is that you lease a mile or so of river, build yourself a sluice, or use an old one, and hope that a nugget or three will flow into your 'pan'. Michael got enough in a fortnight to cover the costs and a bit beyond and I got enough to fill a small tooth cavity, but it was nice and cool, half in and half out of the flowing water most of the day.

I soon found out the drill in this so-called hotel which if my memory will stand the strain was called 'Mon Repose' which name was quite apt, for every night there was a dance and you chose your girl from the many that there were there, danced with her, bought her a drink and if you liked her, you popped the question which was generally "Yes, lead on mate".

Sydney lasted about a week. I guzzled oysters at a dinah (shilling) a dozen, surfed on the famous Bondi Beach which was glorious, and one day 'Mother' called me to the desk and explained that I had better leave on the morrow as the money I had given her was about to run out.

And so I found myself back on the cattle station, telling my old mates what I had been up to. I dealt with some more Morse signals for the boss and was then asked whether I would volunteer to mend and replace a line of fencing that the kangaroos had broken down some 25 miles to the west of the station and I would make up a team with two others who had done the job before. The pay was a 'dinah' a post, driven in and with two barbed and one plain wire and bracing rails every 50 yards.

So off the three of us went the next day with one rifle between us to shoot game for food, spades, axes, saws, staples and rolls of wire, and gelignite. The usual swag was tied and rolled behind our saddles and of course the usual lariat, which with a lot of practice I was just starting to use with some effect.

We soon came to the first break which was a sad sight, for three kangaroos had attempted to leap the fence and all three were entangled. Two were dead and the third was with young in pouch, but dying, so we shot her. I tried to save her young but to my surprise found that this tiny mite, no longer than my thumb nail, had its head actually fused to the teat of his mother and when I did eventually pry him loose, there was blood on his tiny mouth. I kept him alive, wrapped up in a handkerchief and fed him on dried milk and water for three days but he died. I have often wondered how that minute object was able to reach the pouch, let alone be able to attach himself by a sort of skin graft to the teat.

I learnt fairly soon why we were carrying sticks of Gelignite, for some of the ground where we had to re-erect a new fence was *rock*, and we had to drill a hole in the rock about twelve inches deep and place a stick of Gelly in the hole, and then insert either a slow fuse (green) or a red fuse which was a lot quicker, light the fuse and retire rapidly to a safe distance. There would be a puff of smoke, a bit of a bang and then there was a neat hole for a new fence post. We lined it up accurately with the line of the fence, wedged up the base with shivers of blown up rock and there was another 'dinah' to be shared between the three of us.

My two mates soon found that they were a damn sight better with an axe than I was, so I dug most of the holes and they supplied the newly axed stakes and then we joined forces, applied the wire, put the strainers on and drove in the staples.

We did this job for some two weeks, counted up the posts we had done and notched each one with our combined brand so that if anyone wanted to check our work, they could.

During the time that we were away, we seemed to live on wild pig, which were abundant, although somewhat tough to chew. Although we carried quite a lot of food in tins, there was a limit as to how much we could load onto pack ponies. When we ran out, I used to be sent out by the other two, for although they could use an axe, I seemed to be a lot better with a rifle, so pig and bush turkeys would be brought back by this young Pommy to the camp fire. When we were lucky enough to make camp by a large water-hole, there would be crayfish to catch which were first rate eating, although my two companions were a bit wary of them at first till they saw that I was still alive the next morning.

Catching crayfish demanded a whole heap of patience. I tied a lump of meat onto a length of string, say about 20 foot and threw it in and watched through the crystal clear water as a crayfish became interested, and as he put a claw out to grab it, I pulled the bait just a little bit closer to the shore. When I had our future supper about a yard away I kept as still as the flies would allow — for they came in their hordes over any human face — and allowed the 'cray' just a small nibble, just to give him some idea how this bit of meat actually tasted, and then he would put out a large claw to grab the meat and that was the time when I hoicked him out of the water and onto the bank.

We boiled them in our long suffering billy-cans, I say long-suffering, for we used them for everything. We brewed our tea in them, boiled spuds and shaved in them. We didn't shave often because the more hair we had on our faces the less the flies annoyed us. And so the three of us wended our way home, richer by quite a few pounds, the horses in good fettle and ready for whatever came our respective ways.

By this time I had been over a year on the place and had learned to ride a horse fairly well, although I would never match the skills of the other stockmen. I could use a 21 foot stock whip as well as the next. I could rope a young steer at full gallop and had been on mustering round-ups. I had broken to a saddle some four wild horses and my 21st birthday was looming and then came the episode of Archie.

His name wasn't really Archie but that was what he was called and he was a half cast, generally a nice enough sort of bloke, moody at times, but that was caused by the behaviour of his *lubra* (Aboriginal woman). According to Archie she was his property, although she often had other ideas on that subject and would, without a further thought end up in anyone's bed. There were rows and fights between the two of them and one day, late in the evening Archie had had enough, so he broke into the Manager's store, *borrowed* a Winchester and a bottle of whisky, saddled-up and rode off into the night.

We didn't actually miss him 'till the next afternoon, when he should have been found doing a certain job, so enquiries were started and the picture became clearer — Archie had gone 'bush'.

The Manager called us together and explained the situation which meant that if we did nothing, Archie would be dingo meat within the next two to three days. We didn't really have much choice. He was a human being. A bit of a twit at times, but likeable, so we saddled-up. No pack ponies though, for we would have to travel fast in the cool of the very early morning, rest up in the heat and saddle-up again in the evening.

We carried everything that we thought we would need, including Winchesters, water and some food, and set off that same evening at a slow canter. The Australian horse is actually called a 'waler', and has the nicest and most comfortable slow canter you could ever wish for, helped no end by the shape and size of the Australian outback saddle which had about a 6″ dip and two leather knobs, for want of a better description, which fitted nicely just in front of your inner thigh.

We took turns in following Archie's tracks which were plain to see, even in the gloom , and we made camp that evening at about 23.00 hrs, brewed up, had a smallish bite and into our swag, for the nights, unlike the days were inclined to be chilly to a degree.

As usual I was shaken awake and I rounded up the five horses, comfortably riding mine without a saddle, unlike a year ago when I kept on sliding off. Another brew-up and off we set long before the dawn was breaking, again finding the tracks and also where Archie had camped on his first night.

On we rode, found some shade at midday and rested up till about 17.00 hrs, where once again we followed dear Archie. It was about 19.00 hrs when it was quite plain that Archie's horse had taken a tumble, perhaps through fatigue, but all we knew was that none of the tracks were made by a walking horse, they were all at a fast lope and no horse can go on mile after mile in that fashion, especially in the heat of the day.

The second night was a repeat of the first and again as dawn was coming up we started and almost at once we found Archie's horse, dead with a bullet through his brain and a broken foreleg and a few hundred yards further on in Archie's footprints, we found his rifle.

Now our trouble really started for Archie was heading for rock and following his footprints became more and more difficult. It was decided that we would split up and ride till 12.00 hrs and if we hadn't found him then we must return home or otherwise there would be seven corpses out in this rocky desert in place of one, for our water supply was getting to the point of no return.

I remembered waving to the others as we set out in just slightly different directions. I walked my horse carefully amongst the flat rocks that abounded and sweated, and sweated, for we were really riding at a time when the sun was approaching its hottest and we should have been holed up in some shady spot. The horizon at times became blurred but no sign of what must now be either a corpse or a stumbling figure and *I WENT TO SLEEP.*

I woke up, still in the saddle, to find my horse stumbling and my Stetson over my eyes so that the nape of my neck had had the full blast of the noon day sun, for how long I have no idea, and worse thing of all, pulling my compass out of my pocket, I saw I was heading in quite a different direction to the one that I had started. I reined in and realized that my horse was trembling with exhaustion and the poor old girl was, like her rider on her last legs.

Now in the desert in an emergency, there is always the safety precaution that if you fire your rifle TWICE the others would converge on you to see what the problem was. So not without some effort I pulled the Winchester out of its holster, injected a shell into the breech, pulled the trigger, repeated the whole thing and waited for figures to emerge from the blazing desert.

Nothing happened. How long I waited and waited, I have no idea and then I realized that I was going to die. Die on my 21st Birthday, for last night my mates gave me a 21st birthday present by the light of the flickering camp fire. They each tipped just a few drops of their precious water into my billy and in spite of my protests made me drink it and we were *VERY* short of water.

24

I had long since stopped sweating, itself a danger point and I must admit I was frightened. I even thought of putting a bullet into poor old Shirley's head and following up with one into mine but for some reason or other balked at the idea. How long I and my horse stood there I have no idea, but I was wakened by the sound of a horse's hooves on rock, and so was Shirley. She had heard this sound as well, but what was more than surprising was that it sounded as though the horse was shod.

I looked tiredly round the hazy horizon but saw nothing. I thought that I might pump another shot into the air but found that the effort of dragging the rifle out of its holster was too much for me, but Shirley moved off in the direction which *she* thought the other horse was going to appear, and I was past caring. I swayed in the saddle and somehow or other held on, for if I had fallen off I certainly would never have got mounted again.

And so we slowly stumbled for what seemed hours till suddenly there was a shout and there to my misty eyes appeared five horsemen and on the back of the last one, with his head lolling, was in fact Archie and he was still alive.

I was greeted with the usual good humoured banter and asked them where the other rider had come from and did we know him.

"What other rider?" says the head stockman. "Nobody else would be fool enough to come into this God forsaken place."

I rode on, thankful to be with humans that I knew and liked, but as I rode I wondered, and am still wondering who would ride a shod horse in the middle of a bloody great rocky desert. *He* was alleged to have ridden a mule and that *must* have been shod!

It was a month or two after the Archie episode when a galaxy of trucks arrived at the station to sink a bore hole some 30 miles north of us where water was short and another well needed to be found and bored. A vast tank was to be erected, a windmill installed with cattle troughs leading off from the tank.

Just as they were about to set off, one of the gangers, as they were called fell ill with suspected appendicitis. I Morsed a sort of Mayday signal, a plane landed, the man concerned left and that was that bar for the fact the gangers were a man short and could the Manager suggest anyone suitable who would be willing to 'have a go'. So it had to me, why I cannot think, but perhaps because I am always more than willing to learn something I know nothing about.

The head ganger viewed me with some suspicion. "A Bastard Pommy," said he, "can you drive a truck?" "Too right," I said which is true Oz for "Yes, of course I can," and I was shoved into the back of a truck with my swag and all my other very small worldly possessions and off we set into the desert with my two other companions also viewing me with some suspicion for the Oz just doesn't believe that anyone can talk as a "Bastard Pom" can.

I was heading into quite a different mode of living as we no longer slept under the stars. We had tents. Even a sort of camp bed and as for the cooking — no longer were a handful of twigs set alight by twizzling a stick round another stick — we had *matches* and a portable gas stove and saucepans. My billy-can which I insisted I kept, was viewed with some misgivings that their new man might fall sick, drinking out of a blackened object like that.

The whole project oriented round a man called Rush. He didn't appear to have a first name. He was called Rush and that was that, for he was the *dowser* and the whole expedition depended on Rush finding water.

There was one slight snag, for Rush was a drunk and I wondered at the time why he was ever employed. Although he was a bottle a day man he and I got on very well and he encouraged me to walk with him when he was actually dowsing, so in time I started to wonder how it was all done. Rush would wander along in a seemingly aimless fashion, holding a forked stick in both hands and would suddenly stop and the stick would bend down towards the earth. Rush would mutter. "That's no bloody good," and wander on.

One day, it must have been the third or fourth day that we had set out, Rush called to me and said. "Come on son, see if you can do what I am doing," and he handed me a spare stick, showed me how to hold it and told me to walk in a certain direction. Suddenly the stick that I was holding developed a mind of its own and although I tried to stop it, it bent down till I thought it would break.

Underneath where it had bent I suddenly saw one of Rush's

markers, which meant that I was getting the same reaction as he did. I could dowse, and I really felt that I had achieved something. Rush was pleased and off he went back to the camp and told the foreman that the lad (me) would, in time be as good as he was.

Rush continued with his bottle a day and one morning it became apparent that he wouldn't be doing any more dowsing, for he was dead. We buried him deep out in the desert and cut a branch to mark the grave. As best I could, I carved *"RUSH — Dowser"*, on the stick.

In his few sober moments Rush used to talk to me like a father to a son, although he would never talk to any of the other Gangers, because I think he got fed up with always being told that he was a hopeless drunk. Of course he was, but he was an educated man. He'd been to a good school in Australia and had, according to him, made a fortune and lost it. He never said how he lost it, and I didn't enquire for it wasn't my business, which I think he appreciated.

He also told me where he was intending to find a large amount of water, but he wouldn't know the exact spot till he found two large hills forming a valley. It was at the bottom of this valley, where it spread out onto a large plain, that water in vast quantities would be found and he gave me the compass bearing on which he was heading.

That evening the head ganger called us all round and said that as that drunk Rush had let us down, we had better pack everything up and head back. It was then that one of the gangers mentioned the thought that "our Pom" (he meant me) must know something of the art of dowsing, Rush had said so, and he was sober at the time, so why not spend a few more days and let him have a go?

So it was decided, not without some misgivings from some of them, to give young Geoffrey a chance. Three days, they said, and if no water then we turn back.

The next morning, me for once in the lead truck and with Rush's compass firmly clutched in my hot hand off we set. It wasn't all that easy driving what used to be called a Diamond T truck which had, at a rough guess, some 16 gears. With a bit of luck it would change from four wheel drive to two wheel drive when the sand got firm enough, otherwise it was a somewhat slow march forward in four wheel drive and hope that you didn't get bogged down, which made the driver (me) somewhat unpopular as the rest of them had to dig me out.

The first day we found nothing, just flat sandy country, but on the second day we were found, so to speak, by some 'walk about' Abbos and I got into a conversation with them just in case they knew where these two hills were situated. They numbered about sixteen in all and one of them could talk a sort of English (or maybe Australian). The men were naked and the women wore a loin cloth, but nothing else and I must admit the sight of some of those breasts, uptilted and proud, made my young heart beat a bit quicker than usual. When I explained what I was looking for there was an excited jabber in their native tongue and I was told that particular area was sacred to their tribe and no white man should enter otherwise there would be trouble.

But they possibly somewhat inadvertently pointed me in a slightly a different direction to the one that Rush had given me, and when they had left, I altered my compass bearing just slightly to take in their new sighting.

Once again we set of. Ahead I had some 50 hours of driving the lead truck and getting out and fiddling about with my dowsing stick and if we didn't find anything, then back we would go with a mob of very annoyed gangers, for their wages were linked to the prospect of finding water. No water, no big wages.

Down to the last 24 hrs and I really felt guilty. Here was I, a mere 21 year old youth leading three vast trucks and half a dozen grown men on what might turn out to be a complete wild goose chase and all hinging on the last spoken words of a habitual drunk.

It was in the afternoon of the last day that we sighted some hills, and I urged on my ancient four wheeler with the vain hope that I might see *two hills* side by side, forming a valley. Then, out of the heat of the semi scrub cum grassland round us came the shape of first one hill and then another and they seemed to flow down like a mirage and at the bottom just as Rush had said was a green valley.

We ground to a halt and I leapt out, my dowsing stick at the ready, quite expecting it to twitch and bend for me, but nothing. I was being watched closely by all my ganger mates and I could almost feel the groan of disappointment when yard by yard I went across that little valley with my stick thrust out in front of me. Still nothing. Then, as I was about to turn and take another slant, there came a movement in my stick — not a lot — but there was something. I marked that spot and walked on and suddenly I was almost pulled onto my face. The pull was enormous. I couldn't hold it.

Retrieving my stick I went back a bit and again advanced towards that spot, having shaken the stick against my leg as was taught to me by my drunken friend. Again the same exercise was repeated, so I marked it out with a circle of sticks and went back to the foreman who was waiting with some impatience for me to report.

I told him I had found a mass of water, how deep I didn't know but thought that it was well over one thousand feet. "Bloody hell," said the foreman, "are you sure?"

"Yes," I said, "there is water there."

And so we set up the drilling gear and away we went with a six inch bore, lining as we went with steel core and at 850 feet or thereabouts, just when some of my mates were starting to look at me, we struck and a huge great 'gusher' which pushed its head into the sky, soaking everyone, but that didn't matter, we had found and struck water and that was worth £100 or more to each one of us.

We had some fun capping the bore, there was such pressure, but finally it was well and truly controlled and we built the 50 foot tall derrick over it with a six bladed wind vane to pump out the water when the pressure subsided and then the vast round metal holding tank. I have not the slightest idea how much it held, but it was about 30 feet across and we all bathed in it, which was a delight after all the blazing sun.

Six cattle troughs were then arranged round the tank and that was that until some blacks came along and made it clear they didn't like the idea of this strange 'God' with waving arms, but the dogs they had with them plunged one by one into the cattle troughs, which seemed to reassure them that we had not created evil.

So we all went back via the cattle station and I was dropped off with a lot of thanks from my Ganger mates and they returned down to the coast whence they had come.

I was greeted with the news that we had another Pommy with us, and would I bloody well do something about him for they all loathed the sight of him. I went and found him and I must say, with the deepest respect to my fellow countrymen, that this chap — who was blessed with the name of Percy — was ill advised to come out to a cattle station. You could tell at a glance. The face, with its pencil-thin moustache, hair slicked back, a shirt with, of all things, a tie, and last, but certainly not least, immaculate jodhpurs and elastic sided polished riding boots.

He first told me that he didn't think much of the bunk-house, would have liked a room to himself, thought the horses were pretty rough and was interested to know who was his groom and what was this tin can thing, pointing at his new billy-can. He went on to say that he had hunted with the H.H. since a boy and was considered pretty good as a horseman.

I asked him whether he had told all this to the other stockmen to which he replied that he thought that he had explained everything quite well to them.

My reply of, "God help you, because I don't think I can," left him puzzled.

I confess that I was quite interested to see how our Percy performed on the next occasion when we all mounted up, and I was not a bit surprised to see Percy fly in the air as soon as he mounted. Someone was doing the old burr trick as happened to me over a year ago, and I wondered what I should do, so went to Syd and told him that he had had his fun for the day and would he now, as a favour to me, stop it. Much to my astonishment he did just that. I helped Percy to his feet, made some excuse to undo his saddle and whipped the offending burr away without him noticing anything.

To give Percy his due he was quite a fair rider, although he rode too short, and I told him so after several miles with his knees tucked up under his chin, and he agreed with me and altered his irons to a comfortable length. A lariat was quite useless to him and he was a positive danger with a stockwhip and not too happy sleeping in a swag and drinking out of a billy. Then after enquiring where the nearest loo happened to be, which kept every stockman in hoots for days on end, he trudged out, as we all did, dug a small hole, attended to the needs of nature and was silent for days.

What finished Percy with the whole idea of Australia in general and this cattle station in particular was his so-called skirmish with a snake. He had been told when he first came out, what to do and what you should not do, and of course he was told about the bite of a snake but one evening, after a hard day rounding up hundreds of head of cattle, we were relaxing by a water-hole and Percy had gone off to see if he could catch a crayfish. Suddenly a galloping horseman appeared in the distance yelling at the top of his voice. It was Percy and when he heaved his sweat stained pony to a halt he exclaimed in a shaking voice that he thought that he had been bitten by a snake.

"Where?" asked the head stockman. "Here," said Percy pointing to his rump. The next thing Percy knew was that we all more or less threw ourselves at him, turned him over on his stomach and much to his embarrassment, whipped off his now somewhat stained jodhpurs, and there it was, two neat little punctures, just the right distance apart for a snake's bite.

"Razor blade, quick, someone," yelled Bill, and someone produced a blade and whilst we all held the struggling Percy, a neat cut was made across the area concerned. Then there was just the slightest pause because we all knew what had to be done next — suck the wound and extract the venom and spit and spit and spit.

"Come on Geoffrey," said Bill, "its a Pommy arse, you get on with it *NOW*," and so I did just that. It was the most unpleasant job I had ever done, for I had to get my nose more or less up Percy's somewhat smelly backside before I could get my mouth over the bleeding wound. At last it was done and I spat out blood and sweat and I hoped, snake venom, for quite a while, washed my face and came back to the now kneeling Percy who was having the wound bound up.

But that wasn't the end of the tale for there is a tradition out in the bush which was that *if* you could find the snake then it *must* be killed and snakes always lie up after the have spent venom. We hoisted the somewhat sore Percy up onto his horse and told him to lead us to where he had been bitten, and off we went.

It was just about here, said Percy, getting off his pony. "What were you doing?" asked Bill. "I was just getting down to get a drink of water from this pool." "Show us," said Bill, and Percy

31

got down and went on one knee and suddenly let out a yell. "There it is again."

It was Percy's rowel at the end of his spur which had dug into his bottom and the thought that he would die had prompted him to gallop back to the camp.

He thought that we were all an unseemly crowd, laughing our respective heads off over his sore bottom and he left us soon after.

I had by this time done over a year on this cattle station and thought, not without some regret, that I ought to leave and learn another sort of farming and answered an advertisement in one of the rare papers that we got. This was a sheep farm in south Australia and they wanted a Jackeroo. Here my Morse came in handy for me, because I radioed down to Brisbane and they kindly phoned these people up who said they would take me on.

So I gave in my notice to the Manager, which required a week and off I set, but before I went the 'lads', with whom I had worked for over a year, gave me a hell of a party and wished me well. I do owe them all a great debt of gratitude for they took a lone Pommy (Bastard) into their private midst and showed me how things should be done in a cattle camp and I really learnt a lot from them. What is more, they rubbed off the bits of a somewhat useless life that I had lead before I came to their shores.

My journey down to south Australia was not without its trauma as I'd hitched a lift on a convenient wool wagon. This was a massive affair with a vast trailer attached behind a 60 foot wagon driven by a huge engine with sixteen gears, eight forward in two wheel drive and eight in four wheel. The driver, nice chap that he was, got so drunk in the first town on our journey and in which we spent the night, that he was unable to drive and was in fact placed in the local hospital.

While I was in the cab waiting for him to turn up the very worried agent of the firm concerned asked whether I could drive. Idiot that I was and still am, I immediately said, "Yes," and was taken on, with no proof that I had an Australian driving licence — which I hadn't — and was promised the vast sum of £5.00 *per day*, if I was able to bring this vast load of wool safely to its destination in Brisbane. That was fine, for although I had never driven anything approaching a lorry, I had at the gentle age of 17 been employed by Billy Cotten to pump the supercharger on his Bentley whilst whirling round the track at Brooklands.

I was the proud owner of a Bullnose Morris, had never had a lesson but was shown what a gear lever and a clutch, together with the accelerator, was supposed to do by an excellent girl friend of mine. I must admit she improved my juvenile education in various other matters as well.

Returning to this vast vehicle which was as far as I remember known as a Diamond T and having spent a whole day in it, I thought that I knew vaguely how it worked. As it never appeared to do more than 100 miles within the day, which meant that as Brisbane was at least 600 miles from where we were, I was married to the vehicle for the best part of a week, I asked this agent, "What about the cost of nights' lodging and fuel?"

"How much do you want?" said he, so nothing daunted and looking as if I did this sort of thing every day, I looked him in the eye and said that £100 might cover it.

"Don't forget to hand in the receipts to the office," said he and rolled off 20 £5 notes, and that was that.

The actual journey had its problems for however hard I tried I could never get the truck into top gear, she just wouldn't take it, the sandy tracks were not hard enough so I settled for 7th gear and generally in four wheel drive.

When at last we actually hit a tarmac road things were a lot easier and in the end I did achieve top gear, but by then I had got through Brisbane traffic, no easy task with this vast long trailer bumbling along behind and trying not to clip pavements and lampposts — there was little change out of the £100.

Having delivered my load and obtained a receipt that the vehicle was not damaged, I went and found out how to get from Brisbane to Adelaide and from there to where this sheep farm was situated.

Being now loaded with cash I opted for a train journey, slept most of the way and after various stops arrived at the farm. This was a little smaller being a mere 10,000 acres as against a million and ¾ acres for my last one.

Here life was much more civilised as one slept in a bunkhouse, with comfortable beds, showers and the tucker was great. No starting work at 04.00 every morning as a leisurely 09.00 hrs start was the norm and except for shearing time, which was more than busy, the work was quite simple.

As I was the junior on this sheep station, I got all the odd jobs such as 'dagging', which started a couple of weeks before shearing time. The job was quite simple but very mucky cleaning up the arse end of every sheep that was going to be sheared by straddling the animal and then cutting off the bits that were smeared with muck with hand or electric shears. I was also given the job of docking tails of new born lambs. This was clean and simple in that you stretched a bit of rubber in the shape of a ring over the tail of the lamb and let go the tension and in a while the tail dropped off.

One of the fascinating things about a sheep station was the sheep dogs who seemed to have a natural instinct to muster sheep. Some dogs took kindly to being the rear dog, others liked to be in front of the mob and others would prefer a flank.

I had been on the place about six months when I had a letter from the parents in which they said they thought war would break out soon and if I wanted to join the BEF and not the AEF, I had better come home. So back I came, landed lean and healthy to be greeted by my mother with a lot of love, but her first question was, "Where did you get those clothes from?" So I was whisked off to Harrods and was bought a new suit, which after some 55 years, I still wear to Church every Sunday.

In 1938/9 England was slowly facing up to the fact that in the not too distant future we would be fighting the Hun once again, and all youngsters such as I were invited to join some sort of volunteer force. Having mucked about in boats all my life, I naturally chose the RNVR and I went down to the Embankment where there was a queue of young men waiting to board a craft to see whether they were fit to be taken into the Navy.

I passed all the medical and my schooling seemed to satisfy their Lordships. Then I was told that my eyes should be tested and I sat in a chair and various colours were presented to me and I was asked to name them. It was then, after some 21 years of life, that I discovered I was colour blind.

"Sorry my boy," said the RN doctor — "next," and that was that — no Navy for me.

My Aunt then came to my rescue for she was quite friendly with a senior rank in the HAC, (Honourable Artillery Company) with its HQ in Finsbury Square and she was able to pull a string or two and I joined that illustrious band in the middle of 1938. The Honourable Artillery Company is the oldest Regiment in the British Army and the senior unit of the Territorial Army...It was the first regiment to be granted by the City of London the privilege of marching through the streets with drums beating, colours flying and bayonets fixed.

I joined the 86th HAC, HAA Regiment RA 274 Battery and after firing countless rounds of AA Ammunition at slow flying drogues towed by intrepid airman off the coast of Wales at a place called Apperporth, we found ourselves in Hyde Park on the day that war was declared.

Sirens sounded about midday and we manned our four 3.7 guns waiting with bated breath to be bombed by the nasty Hun, but not a plane was to be seen, which probably was just as well, for although the guns were first rate, shining in the noon sun, we found that we had been issued with 3" ammunition.

So weeks went by. We were finally issued with our complete uniform down to 'Boots — Army — Gunners for the use of' and marched up and down the parade ground and got to know the *Sutling Room* a lot better than the various ack-ack guns which were intended for us to use with unerring accuracy against German planes who were silly enough to fly over England in general and Armoury House in particular. The Sutling Room was really the Regimental bar and what a grand place it was with Pewter mugs by the score hanging on hooks and one was invited to buy one and have your name, rank and number, etched on the side.

The HAC was one of the most friendly regiments in which I had the privilege to serve my country. We were all gunners, and we rubbed shoulders with Generals of the last war who were also gunners, although some did in fact sport a stripe or two, before they departed to Shrivenham or similar places where one was elevated to the commissioned ranks.

One evening when most of us were imbibing pints in the Sutling

Room, the CO came in, called for silence and then asked for volunteers to join an AA Regiment which was off to France. Hands shot up and in no time at all I found myself in a new regiment, situated in a small village called Query La Motte near Arras in Northern France, guarding the aerodrome that Baron von Richthofen used to use in the first world war. We had 3.7s and Bren guns and I got myself the job as a dispatch rider, firstly riding a Norton, then a BSA and finally an Indian, which was great fun. I had the freedom of the somewhat flat French countryside and, with a bit of wangling, could spend a whole night in Paris, first phoning the HQ that the m/c had broken down, and what did they advise? More often than not they would ask whether I could find myself a bed for the night, to which I would reply that I thought that I might manage and snuggled down with some very nice French girl. Many of them thought it was their bounden duty to entertain these brave lads in Khaki who had come to save them from a fate worse than death.

Then those pleasant times had to cease, for there was a war on, although in our neck of the woods we were enjoying life in no mean way, except for the odd times that the Hun came over their old aerodrome, merely to see whether it was still in being. Then the Hun spoilt it all and broke through the so-called impregnable Maginot line and we and the rest of the British Army headed for points North in general and Dunkirk in particular. The journey to Dunkirk from our point of view was not without its moments. The Hun was never far away and we soon learnt to distrust the good intentions of our Allies, the French, for we would often wake in the morning and find our flank gone, as the French had taken off in the night, God alone knows where, but they left us.

After some few days we arrived at what used to be a nice sea side sandy beached resort called Dunkirk to find it in flames and blackened by blazing oil tanks. We set up our guns and spent hours firing, not without some success, at diving Stukas. When we first arrived we were ordered to ditch all out MT (Motor Transport) into the nearest dock and in went my beloved Indian motor cycle.

Some of us got bored with digging slit trenches in the sands and cowering down every half an hour or so to avoid the bombers. Some clever chap suggested that we retrieve our motor bikes from the sea, clean them up and when we could, have races over the sands — regiment against regiment.

Greatly helped by both the Engineers and REME we got some thirty bikes going and there was this nice Brigadier who somehow or other found a blackboard and chalk and acted as a sort of Bookie and bets were laid as to which Regiment would win the next race — courtesy of the Stukas of course. This is where I came unstuck, for I was in a race of some 25 bikes and was for some reason in the lead, racing over the bomb holed sands. Other bikes were thundering behind me and suddenly right in front of my front wheel appeared a bloody great hole. The Bombers were at it again and with the noise of the bike engines none of us had heard what the rest of the Regiments had..

I woke up to find myself strapped onto a stretcher in an ambulance, with half my face covered up and a filthy pain in my left foot. We were going like the clappers and painfully turning my head around I saw, to my consternation, that the driver was French and that there must have been another ten or so British wounded in the vehicle. I remember arriving at the centre of Dunkirk in the middle of a ghastly air raid with the Hun dropping everything he had in our general direction and the driver, bless him, slammed on his brakes and departed to where he thought was a safer place.

Voices were raised in fright and one asked if there was a driver on board to which, silly me again, I answered that I could drive.

"Well bloody well drive then," everyone shouted, to which I replied that it was a bit tricky because I was strapped in. "Not to worry Mate," and various hands untied my straps, but then the blood, which was held in check by the bandage, started welling up over my eyes and I couldn't see a thing. Someone, I shall never know who, kindly refixed the bandage, wiped the blood out of my eyes and held onto me whilst I struggled to the driver's seat and I was able to see the blurred shape of the road ahead.

And that was how we finally got down to the docks to find a ship waiting. We were helped aboard and laid down in serried rows on the deck. I don't remember much more of the journey till I woke up in Bradford Hospital, listening in wonder to the Bishop of Bradford lecturing us on the immorality of the British soldier, and as the dear

Bishop spoke, a light aircraft passed over head and men slid out of their beds to slip underneath — we disliked the sound of *any* aircraft.

Most of us got better and I was posted back to the HAC, the only one out of 70 volunteers who actually returned, although many might have done later.

I was sent off to Shrivenham to see whether I was good enough to sport pips on my shoulders and after some eight weeks I emerged, with Sam Browne gleaming and was posted to a Maritime Regiment up in Hull. The job was to fix Bofors or even 3″ guns onto the stern decks of merchant ships about to depart and which needed defensive equipment and men to man the guns.

We trained men and installed guns, which sounds easy, but first we had to get a suitable engineer to tell us whether the deck concerned was strong enough to withstand the recoil of a gun. At the start of the exercise we would install what we thought was a suitable weapon, train a crew to man it and politely ask the skipper to take us to sea to make sure the whole thing worked and we had taken suitable precautions to prevent shooting the bridge and all who manned it. What happened once or twice was that when we fired the gun, it, and most of the crew, disappeared through the after deck.

I was then posted as second in command to another Maritime Battery up in Scotland at a place called Loch Ewe. There we had a slightly different job, for there were no docks and we had to take our guns out on lighters to the ships that wanted ack-ack guns, and hoist them on board.

There was a Wrennery on the shore with a lot of WRNS, most of whom were ferried out to ships to sort out their sea telegraphs and codes. They took preference against any 'Brown job' as they described us, and at times there were slight arguments when we were heading for a ship on our slow moving lighter only to be passed by a fast moving launch with a Wren officer on board which meant we had to steam round the ship concerned till the Wrens had finished their job and we had room to get our lighter alongside.

I soon became friendly with a number of Wrens and was often invited to their ward room for drinks and hilarious parties, till one evening in the middle of one of these, a very senior Wren came in and pointing at me implied that this was a Navy Ward Room and that

'Brown Jobs' were not really welcome. She said all this in quite a pleasant fashion and as she was very good looking, I took the hint and left.

As the days went by and work went on I kept on seeing this particular Wren and took great care to salute her, for although I was a Captain at the time, she was in fact senior to me. Finally, with greatly daring I asked her whether she would have dinner with me at the nearest hotel and to my surprise she said that she would love to, so off we went. She perched on the back of a battery motor cycle and we had a great dinner and she allowed me to plant a kiss on her cheek when we said good night.

I was due to depart on a ship to Murmansk in about a fortnight, for this particular craft had ack-ack guns of a new type fitted on board and the powers that be wanted a detailed report on them if and when they went into action.

During this last fortnight this Senior Wren and I went out quite a lot and although I had known a lot of girls in my young life, I had never felt quite like this with any girl and I had the feeling that she felt more than kindly towards me, so on the last night before I sailed on that dreaded trip to Murmansk, I asked her to marry me and to my delight she said she would when I returned from Russia.

Off I set with our new ack-ack equipment, plus four Bofors and some dozen gunners, all from the 4th Maritime Regiment, but half way to Iceland all our engines packed up. We were looked after by a minute minesweeper, whilst the rest of the convoy sailed on but we spent an unpleasant 24 hours with the vessel wallowing in the very cold sea till our engineers got one engine going and we limped back to Ault Bay and Loch Ewe.

As soon as I got ashore, I departed to find my fiancée, saluted her with a smile and when nobody was looking, a lingering kiss and asked when she could get some leave, for I felt that we ought to get wed as soon as possible to enjoy what might be a somewhat short married life. I had no knowledge when I might be dispatched to Russia, and the odds on returning in one piece were somewhat short. Thalia Cooper and I wangled 72 hours leave and departed to London to be joined together according to the Church, for I was determined that we would have a Church wedding. With a lot of telephoning we got permission from the Archbishop of Canterbury's office to be wed in the Church at the top end of Roehampton Lane in London. Why there in particular? Firstly Thalia, although British had been born in Chile, where her father was a British Consul, and secondly my mother and step-father lived in a block of flats called Fairacres which is situated in Roehampton Lane.

The journey down from Scotland to London was not without its problems, for having departed in somewhat of a rush, we found that there wasn't a seat to be had on the train. We were ushered into the guards van which was full of gun toting redcaps guarding a consignment of gold bullion, who regarded us with deep suspicion. We found a sort of a seat and settled down for the night but I was woken up by my future wife who demanded to know where the 'loo' was situated? This question posed somewhat of a problem for there wasn't a loo, not even a bucket and I discovered that the redcaps had been lowering a window on the 'lee' side so to speak and dangling 'John Thomas' into the breeze and letting fly. This was reasonably easy for the males but females are built in a different fashion and I had to 'shoo' the redcaps out of a portion of the carriage and my future wife divested herself of the lower clothes, I heaved her rear portion out of the lowered window and hanging on for dear life, ordered her to 'let fly'. This was quite a success, although Thalia's rear portions were somewhat chilled in the night air.

And so we arrived in London, grabbed a taxi and dashed to Roehampton Lane so that my mother could meet her future daughter in law, always a good thing to do, and then further scampering round London to obtain our special licence. On the way in the middle of Picadilly Circus, in a traffic jam up, Thalia suddenly screamed that there was Peter, one of her many first cousins, who also had come over to join up, so we hauled him in to our cab, didn't tell him what we were up to for time was of the essence, dropped Peter, grabbed the Licence and sped back to the Church at the top of Roehampton Lane. Here mother was waiting with my best man, the Brigadier in charge of the four Maritime Regiments who had kindly consented to do the honours on my behalf, but we wanted one more witness and so I dashed out and asked a passing male whether he would mind stepping into the breach. And so the Leets and the Coopers became one and we hired a car. During the war the maximum round journey was 72 miles and so we stayed at a delightful small hotel called the Hautboy at Ockham in Surrey till the time came for us to both depart, now as man and wife, back to the wilds of Scotland in general and Loch Ewe in particular.

There were no married quarters up in Loch Ewe, so we were more or less divorced after our 72 hours honeymoon. Then Thalia was posted to Glasgow and there we obtained a small flat, and most week ends I was able to get away and join my wife in somewhat noisy Glasgow.

Some decent period after we had been wed it became apparent to the powers that be on the female side of the Navy that my wife was pregnant, and with some reluctance she was posted to Civvy street.

By this time I had left the Maritime Regiment and was posted to Rye where we had the undoubted pleasure of being presented with the best target that any ack-ack gunner could wish for in the shape of the doodle bug. Constant height, constant speed and constant direction and our best performance on our particular front was 124 shot down within twenty four hours.

We were able to rent a small house in Church Square in Rye and I could turn my predictors round and view my now somewhat large wife tending our minute garden in which wandered our two hens, Henerietta and Harriet, who willy-nilly gave us a couple of eggs per day. Came the time when the birth was imminent and Thalia departed to Slough in Bucks where she presented me with a charming daughter all of 9 lbs. Shortly afterwards Hitler decided that enough was enough and war was ended.

We then had to decide how we would earn the necessary pennies to keep body and soul together. As far as we could see, we could depart to Australia, where I had had a finger in quite a few farming pies *or* we could go in quite the opposite direction and try Chile.

Thalia had been born in that country. Her father, Edward Cooper, was a British Consul there, and so we were presented with some 10,000 acres of farm land by the kindness of the Cooper family, and off we set on an ex troop ship, the three of us, laden with nappies for our young daughter. Husbands and wives were separated, the wives having to live and bunk in one vast area, and many of them had babes in arms. Their nights were somewhat noisy for one baby would wake another, and did they yell.

And so we arrived in Buenos Aires and there struck a slight snag, because I was obliged to wear my British uniform when I turned up at my final destination and the Argentineans disliked the sight of anything dressed in Khaki.

The reason I was in uniform stemmed from the fact that I had joined up from Australia and not from England and therefore HMG in their kindness paid for my passage back to wherever I wanted, be it Australia, or in this case Chile. They kindly included my wife plus children that had been gathered on the way. For a day or so before we could get a train departing over the Andes to Chile, I was often elbowed off the pavement by irate Argentineans, till I started to do some elbowing on my own account and that stopped the rot.

So we embarked on the train which climbs about 13,000 feet and where one does not want to take a lot of exercise as the air is so rarefied.

We arrived in Chile to find a lot of Thalia's relatives interested to see what she had picked up out of the British Army and of course what we had produced between us in the shape of our daughter, Jennifer.

My new father-in-law then threw a large party in which I was introduced to the Chilean drink called Pisco which is the distillation of grape skins and whilst it tastes like pleasant water, it has a kick like ten mules. As the last guest said farewell, I passed out flat on the floor of the British Consulate.

Two days later we set off for our new farm called San Sebastian, with the house set up on a tall hillside overlooking the San Pedro river and the background of the snow capped Andes made a wonderful setting.

We were slightly worried to be told on our arrival that the last major-domo had been shot dead on the doorstep of the farm-house a couple of weeks previously — we never knew who was responsible. The new major-domo was a trifle disconcerted to find that his new boss's knowledge of the language was more or less nil, but as time went by, and with the help of my wife and an English/Spanish dictionary, I began to converse and understand what they were all talking about.

The farm-house had a tin roof, no water, no light and a wood stove for cooking *but* we appeared to have many servants, at least three in the house and about 80 on the farm. The whole set-up was somewhat feudal which I found somewhat disturbing. I was not used to having men bow to me and women curtsey and I soon found out that El Patron (me) was not supposed to lift a hand to actually do any work.

We also had a slight worry in that on one of our borders lay a small coal mine and the miners had the habit of cutting my boundary wire at night, ushering in their stock to feed off my grass, and then whiping them out before it was light.

I called on the mine overseer and asked him to stop this habit, to which he shrugged and said that as it was the custom, he could do nothing. I got someone to print out a notice in Spanish which read, 'Keep your stock out' or words to that effect, and hung it on my fence, facing the mine. Nobody took any notice of this, so I put up another notice which read that I would personally shoot any foreign stock that I found on my land at night. I then lay up on the roof of a shed, overlooking the area concerned, well wrapped up, with a .222 rifle and waited. Came midnight and the sound of stock being moved up to my fence, the clipping sound of wire being cut and in the stock came, all goats. I shot three in quick succession and all hell broke loose with men running hither and thither, but all the stock were taken out, including the three dead animals.

I had an unpleasant half an hour the next day because I thought that it might help matters if I offered to pay for the animals that I had shot, so went down to the mine and passed through ranks of very annoyed miners on the way to their office, but nobody raised a hand. I paid over some money and that was that. My fence stayed upright and my grass grew — my major-domo was astounded.

The next problem was again to do with a neighbour, but this time he was a rich neighbour and he coveted my port. Let me explain. Out of the 10,000 acres we had some 400 acres of virgin forest which was so thick we couldn't ride a horse through, and I thought why not cut trees down, drag them down to the river by bullock, build a raft and float it down to Valdivia and sell the wood.

To do so meant I had to build myself a small harbour, so I started on this project with the aid of a somewhat puzzled major-domo and a dozen men. With the aid of some sticks of gelignite, about which I knew something from my Australian days, I soon had an area in which I could build a decent sized raft. Fine, I thought, till one day my major-domo came along and told me that we had *lost* our port as my neighbour had moved my boundary fence so that the port was now in *his* land.

In my luggage when I arrived in Chile was a 9 mm Luger and about 100 rounds of ammunition. I pocketed the automatic pistol and told my m-d to gather up 12 large men on 12 large horses, a lot of rope and to follow me. When we arrived at what had been my port I found the opposition lined up on the other side of the wire, so shouted "bugger off my land," and waved a hand, thinking they would understand that sort of language, but their head man started to come towards me on his horse. I put three carefully aimed rounds between his horse's legs and that was enough. They were quite prepared to cope with their own kind but *not* a mad gringo who actually shot at them. So we moved our fence back to where it had been, and once again we had a port. I had no more trouble from that direction.

So we farmed. We grew quite a bit of corn, milked about 50 cows and from their produce made cheese, which we sold in our own farm shop. We had about 700 goats, which I didn't like, but we had to have them by law because some years ago some idiot German, I think it was ,who liked eating blackberries came to settle in Chile and he imported some canes. Unfortunately he didn't eat enough, so the canes spread and in the end became a danger to the whole of the country. The blackberry had to be kept down, and in fact we could be fined if we didn't. The easiest way was to fold goats onto a patch of land till the blackberry was eaten down to its roots.

I then got into trouble with the law and two carabineros came up to the farm and very politely, invited me to ride with them down to the nearest court, a distance of some 25 miles. I asked what the trouble was and they replied in unison, "Beans Senor, your families have made a complaint against you that you have changed their beans."

Sounds daft but that's what it was all about. Although we paid our men in cash every week, we also *gave* them a ration of beans — it was the custom — and one day looking at the beans that I had in store to weigh out to each family I thought that they looked pretty rotten. I thought I could get a better type so I sent a couple of men out to get some. This they did and returned with what I thought was a far superior bean but the families took a dim view and some of them complained to the police, hence my visit to the local Court. Into the dock I marched and someone told the Judge, that I was El Capitano Leet. They stuck the Captain part on for it was stamped into my passport. The charge was read out and I was asked whether I thought that I was guilty of this offence or not. I replied that I must be, or words to that effect and explained in my poor Spanish what had happened.

The Judge waved me to silence, and then quite out of the blue, asked me what I was a Captain of?

"A Gunnery Captain, Senor," I replied.

"What sort of guns?" asked learned Judge, and then I thought about such nasty things as the Official Secrets Act, and should I tell him that I had dealt with anything from a Bren gun to a 14-inch naval gun, so I said, "3.7 Senor."

"How interesting," said the Judge. "I belong to the Chilean Volunteer Army, and I also use a 3.7. The case is dismissed. Perhaps you would care to join me in my chambers?

And that was that. We partook of a glass or two and discussed guns. The Judge was very keen on guns.

So life went on, perched above a blue river with the snow capped Andes in the not so far distance.

My parents came out while my step-father was on one of his usual world business tours of the many factories he owned. He was a man of strict habits and always wore a bowler hat and there perched on a somewhat slow moving bullock cart came my mother and step-father with bowler hat still perched on his greying locks. We made them both welcome and that evening before we all went to bed I handed over my Luger to my somewhat astonished step-parent and told him that if anyone came through their front window, shoot first and I will ask the questions later.

Then came the Communists and a good friend of mine, who was very close to the Chilean Government, rang me up one evening and explained the position, and so with some reluctance we decided to sell the place and return to the UK. It was rumoured that foreigners would be turfed off their land and given 1939 prices, less 10%, which would have meant a vast loss. We sold to a German who, apparently, had not heard of this new idea, and I didn't really think it was my duty to tell him.

So we returned whence we came to find my step-father frantic to find a farm manager to run his four hundred acres in Hampshire. Someone had told him that he should buy a farm to avoid paying too much tax on his quite vast income. He had bought one soon after he and mother came out to see us, and had tried out various farm managers only to find that they either rooked him left right and centre, or even worse, thought he knew nothing of farming — and how right they were.

He asked me if I would like to take on this magnificent task and run his acres for him, and for ten very long years I did just that, but to any aspiring young farm manager, I do not recommend that you do the same. One of the many snags to arise is when you have a 20 acre field of wheat and your boss asks you what profit he will make out of it when you have finished the ploughing, the cultivating, the sowing, the combining, the drying, the baling and you are fool enough to give him a figure. Three days before the combines are due to start, the Heavens open and you lose half of it — *AND IT'S YOUR FAULT.*

The business man, unlike the farmer, knows to a penny or so what he is going to make on whatever he manufactures. The farmer, on the other hand is, to a certain extent, under the thumb of the weather....*AND ITS YOUR FAULT.*

Then take the humble cow. "How much milk is she going to give you? Don't you know?" asks my step pa. "And how much will it cost to feed her, and what is the end result. *DON'T YOU KNOW?"*

Quite useless explaining to a business magnate that during the spring and summer months, this non-complaining cow could well give you 3 to 4 gallons per day off the grass *alone*, with a mere pinch of bought in grub. But during the winter months she, not without some effort on her behalf, is giving you 1-2 gallons and expecting at least 3-4 lbs of bought in food for anything extra that she might pass on into the milking machine that's quite a different story. Also it takes quite a bit of time to educate your rich boss that a cow has to calve first before she gives you a pint of milk, and then asks the boss *why* are you selling that *nice* bull calf for only 5/- in the local market where all the bidding *must* be rigged. (My phrasing, not his.)

And pigs — of which we had some 30 sows — and invariably one would lay on an inoffensive piglet which had to be thrown out for the owner of the Rolls to cast his eye upon, and I would be expected to write a letter of apology.

I was a member of the National Farmers' Union and they obviously got a bit short of Chairman for the local branch and willy-nilly I was elected and enjoyed my year in the Chair and hope that I was able to assist in some small way. But according to my good boss it was wasting *his* time, mucking about with a load of farmers from 8 p.m. at night to sometimes 11 p.m., when I could have been doing some office work and earning my princely wage of £12.00 per week — out of which we had to buy a house!

I stood this for ten years and then gave in my notice, and as I was paid by the week, I thought that a notice of a week was about right, but step-pa thought nothing of this and persuaded me to stay till he found an *expert* to replace me, to which I agreed with the proviso that I could have two days off during the week to look for a farm of my own. This was reluctantly agreed, but he hinted darkly that I would be broke within a year and it would be very doubtful that he would have me back.

One day a chap strode into the farm office and stated that he would be taking over from me, handed me a letter from the boss confirming this and requested me to show him what I did every day.

He was very well dressed, and looking at his pristine well manicured hands, I wondered what working knowledge he had of farming. So I told him to meet me at 07.00 the next morning in the yard.

He turned up at 07.30 dressed overall, so to speak and I pointed to a large tractor and a 4–furrow mounted plough and requested him to join them up and I would be back in five minutes. He looked quite blank and asked if I expected *HIM* to actually use this machine *and* plough with it.

I always enjoyed ploughing; in fact I have a brace of cups that I won in a field of about fifteen in a ploughing match, and although I did not win I did come second on two occasions. It is such a nice pastime, as long as you know what you are doing, you have bolted on four nice new points, the sun is shining and the gulls are waiting.

Now the field that we were supposed to have ploughed by the week-end was still lying fallow when my step-pa demanded to know *why* this job hadn't been done. I explained carefully that his new manager was not able to plough, or for that matter, said I somewhat slowly, do *anything* that I generally did, such as milking sixty cows on the cowman's day off, mucking out 30 sows and feeding all round on the pigman's day off, ploughing most of 200 acres of arable and what is more Sir, he doesn't understand the way we keep our books. I always called him Sir, when on duty, which was all the time.

"Rubbish," said my step-pa, "leave it to me, you can now leave". And after a pause — "Good Luck." Which was kind of him.

Now I was more than careful when handing over the petty cash to the New Manager, the books were right to a penny and I had got the boss's signature to that effect. I was just a trifle surprised that evening when the new manager took my wife and I out to dinner as a sort of thank you gesture to me and paid the bill with a roll of notes with my step-father's paper band round it. Nothing to do with me, thought I, but as we departed to our new farm down in Kent, having sold the house, I did wonder how things would be, until I received a phone call from an irate parent accusing me of stealing his duffel coat. "Not guilty," said I, and left it at that, but four months later I heard that the new manager was in court accused of stealing cattle from my dear step parent, and what is more he appeared in the dock wearing the old man's duffel coat.

So once again we were all on our own. Our numbers had now increased by a very nice son, Richard, and I was determined to succeed on this farm of 320 acres, somewhat hilly, but good barley growing land and plenty of good pasture. We arrived with two heifers and a dozen hens, a large mortgage fixed at 3½% and not a lot in the bank. Our bank manager was a kindly soul, and we got on well together and he lent me as much as he could, with which we bought quite a lot of the better stock that the out-going farmer was selling.

I was kept more than busy, for in the start I could not afford any staff, although we had two cottages for workers which we hoped to fill.

I had one tractor and a trailer and would start milking our herd at 05.00, put the churns out by 07.00 and cut kale by hand to feed the cows and be back in our vast old manor house by 08.00 feeling very hungry. I would read the mail during breakfast and put most of it in one of my three trays in my office, one marked action *now*, another pending, and the last one, *done with — file*. The idea was fine, but the action tray got fuller and fuller for I never seemed to have the time to get round to the office.

The cows, dear things, wanted milking in the afternoon as well as the morning, and I would be ploughing or something similar between 09.00 and 13.00 when I would bring tractor and plough back to the house. Viewing my bank statements one day I could now see black figures and thought that with a bit of luck the red ones would disappear soon, so I advertised for a man who could milk and knew something about sheep and pigs. Although at the time I had only cows, I realized in the near future I must start another side-line.

A lot of men applied and I insisted on interviewing the wives as well, for I have found that if the wife does *not* like the house then she is going to be unhappy, and if she is in that state then the husband will be too.

Then sheep. How would he *know* that a ewe had been mounted by a ram, and how would he dag? Could he shear?

Pigs. What weight gain would he expect per pound of food fed in, say a week.

Then if I found a wife who actually liked the house, I had to test the man out. Could he actually milk a cow? How much concentrates would he feed in the winter and for that matter, how much in the summer, per gallon produced?

Lastly I would invite him to back the tractor onto the trailer and lift it up by the hook and then back the lot through that gate. I was not interested in whether he could use a plough or any of the arable business, I could cope with all that *and* sow a couple of hundred acres on my own.

I found that 70% of the applicants merely wanted a free house, which went with the job and most of the wives loathed the very idea of living in the country, so I finally came down to one man and his wife plus their two children, and he, bless him did me proud for nearly ten years till he died.

After some two years of farming once again on my own and now with the vast staff of two, I had 150 ewes and about a dozen sows and their litters plus, of course, our cows which had increased in numbers to some 60 plus their various progeny. I then had the mad idea that instead of the Milk Marketing Board buying my creamy milk at about 2s.6d. per gallon, I might sell it direct to the housewife at more than treble that amount.

I began to woo the housewife in her lair, carrying with me a selection of bottles bearing the names of other dairies *but* filled with my morning's milk and when I saw say three or four empty milk bottles on a door-step, I would ring the back door of the house. The wife would regard my somewhat countrified attire of wellies and straw carefully stuck in my cap with some caution and inquire as to my business. I would then wave my bottle of milk in the air, being careful *not* to disturb the cream line and ask her what she thought of that. More than once, the wife concerned would ask what it was I was holding, to which I would reply. "Milk Madam, and all of three hours old." I would then add swiftly, "Do you know how old that 'stuff' is? pointing to her empty bottles.

I took on a full time cowman, purchased a cartoning machine, milk cooler and crates and was soon selling enough to be in profit with the benefit of sales of eggs, logs and farmyard manure.

And of course, Mrs Smith or Mrs Brown, or both, wanted an egg or three, their husbands demanded FYM (Farm Yard Manure) for their respective gardens, and as most of them at that time had open fires, a bag of logs would come in handy.

At times we would be invaded by our customers *and* their *dear* children for when I started all this I said, "*Do* come and see how proper milk is produced." Sometimes we were inundated with mothers with kids at foot, and although it was quite an education for some of the younger children, who had not the slightest idea how the contents of their bottle of milk had originated, one had to keep a beady eye on the children who never understood that if you insert your head between a cows hind legs you could land up on the ceiling — cows are a bit fussy that way. Some of the younger mothers, viewing the serried ranks of calves in the calf shed, understood that without them, they would not have any milk.

We always sold more milk at lambing time as I had made it plain that whilst I was more than willing to show *OUR* customers I used to call them clients, at times, they were more than impressed) what we had on show on *their* farm, I was not prepared to do that for somebody who still had that stale white stuff plonked on their doorstep every morning.

Our mums and their children were always fascinated by the antics of our two sheepdogs. I used to pretend to whisper in each dog's ear and off they would go and bring the mob back to our feet and the kids used to try and do the same. Of course, it never worked for them, as the quiet 'getawayback' which I used was the key word for our two dogs.

Occasionally on a so-called 'field day', with 20 or 30 mums and their youngsters milling around the place, I would drop a slight clanger when some slightly older child, viewing our calves, would exclaim in a loud voice, "Where's the bull, mister?" and without thinking I would reply, "It's all AI these days. "What is AI, mister?" would be the response, and I would glance questioningly at the nearest mum who would usually shake her head.

Further revenue came from our milk customers after one of them asked if I knew of a good kennels for their little 'Fido' as they were going away for a couple of weeks, and without thinking much I said that we would look after him and returned to the farm with a brace of dogs which we put with the calves. Both lots of animals at first viewed each other with some suspicion, calves hocks were nipped by dogs, and dogs were butted by calves, after that peace reigned, dogs ever nibbled at the concentrates that were fed to calves.

Eventually the dog business got too big and we had to hire a kennel maid to take them out for exercise, but one day she got nipped in a tender part and departed in high dudgeon. So with fingers crossed we let some 30 dogs out into a well fenced five acre paddock and at first the odd Peke regarded all this freedom with some suspicion but after a day or two, a Peke would trot up to an Alsatian and attempt to smell his behind.

I must say that Pekes took on a whole new image when they were returned to their hearth and home, no longer a somewhat timid animal and barked their respective heads off.

Talking about dogs and their somewhat odd habit of always trying and generally succeeding in smelling any strange dog's bottom, have you ever considered why they do it?

It goes like this.

> The dogs once called a meeting,
> They came from near and far,
> Some came by aeroplane
> and some by motor car.
>
> But before into the meeting house,
> they were allowed to look,
> they had to take their bottoms off
> And hang them on a hook
>
> No sooner were they seated
> Each mother's son and sire
> When a nasty little yellow dog
> Rushed in and shouted, *fire*.
>
> They all got up in frantic haste
> They hadn't time to look
> And each seized at random
> A bottom, from a hook.
>
> They got their bottoms all mixed up
> It made them very sore
> To have to wear a bottom
> That they'd never worn before.

So that is why, today, you see
A dog will even leave a bone
To smell another's bottom
In the hope to find his own.

Sorry about that, got quite carried away, but now you know.

So there we were with a nice healthy bank balance, not a lot but without a doubt, black, and we were getting on nicely with all our customers. We tried to remember their various instructions as to where to leave their particular pint, some insisted on the front door step, others would have theirs on the back doorstep. One or two liked it put in a dog kennel, one of whom forgot one day and inserted a dog in the kennel which had been empty for months — that proved interesting for a moment or two. But even more interesting were the one or two nice young housewives who would say, "The back door is open, love, just pop it into the fridge for me, there's a dear." I was in the middle of doing just that one day when the husband, who had been on night duty, returned and the ensuing conversation had its interesting moments!

In the early days when we started with a mini van and my wife, bless her, drove, whilst I delivered, we did have a bit of a day when the wind blew and whilst I was delivering pints to one house, my wife took a tray of eggs to another and the wind took it out of her hands and the road was covered with egg shells and yolk. Now my young wife, who I love dearly, has the odd habit that other women appear to share in that if you make a mess, you *must* clear it up, so there we were at about 06.00 on our hands and knees cleaning up a Kent Road.

It was about then that our milk business received a well earned boost in that Brands Hatch, the racing circuit which was about three miles away from us put out tenders for milk delivery. We put in a tender for a hundred gallons each race day, which was generally about once a fortnight and to our surprise won it. Most of their race days were on a Saturday on which day we did double deliveries to our customers because we didn't deliver on a Sunday. But it did pose a slight problem. How to deliver 100 gallons to the 'Hatch' in churns, and not bottled, thank goodness and also deliver some

2,000 pints to our Browns and Smiths? Only one thing for it. I had to get up an hour earlier, which I did every Saturday for a while till things changed.

I had to deliver a churn to each of the ten little café's round the track at Brands and it seemed much the best idea if I took our new one ton van actually round the track, and dropped off a churn at each café, *but* there were problems with the security people who guarded the track night and day with men and very large Alsatians. I had some arguments with these people and was even pursued by a horde of dogs when I did at first venture onto the track without their permission, but eventually they saw the wisdom of my thoughts when I unloaded ten full churns of milk on *their* office door step for *them* to deliver. After that I was allowed to trundle round the track, dropping off my churns and heaving them over the fence in front of each little café.

We were now stretched to the limit. I was doing a 90 hour week and starting to feel it. The money *was* rolling in, but something had to give or alter somewhere.

And it came about, so simply. It was a Sunday afternoon and a friend of mine with whom I used to play golf in the days when I had that sort of time, phoned me up and asked whether he could bring his clubs up and a few balls and practice with his new 7 wood because there was a medal on at his Club and he couldn't practise.

"Of course," I said, "I might come and join you, haven't swung a club in years," and so there we were at the entrance to a field. In front of us was a small, well kept wood (even if I say so myself) some 200 yards away and behind that was a bank and then some flat ground, from where we were, say some 450 yards. I cannot remember whether I said it first or my friend did, but maybe we both said it together — *make a bloody good par five this would.*

And then I had this crazy idea — make a golf course — we only had a couple near us, Knowle and Wilderness and Wrotham a bit further away, but you couldn't get in to either of the big ones, they were full to the brim. And all that afternoon, I was thinking and planning.

Where would the first tee be; the tenth MUST be near it, and what about the par of the course; had I enough acres? How many par three's could I fit in? Ideally it should be six three's, six fours, and six fives, and that would be a Par 72. Too long by half, I thought, one wants to attract the man who only has a few hours to spare. Better to try for 70 or even 69. Club House? and then of course the real penny dropped. This place *had* been a golf course years ago and was shut in 1942 because of the war and there was *nothing* left to show that Henry Cotton had actually opened the place all those years ago. There *was* a golf Club House, but it was occupied as a private dwelling so I would have to build another one — nothing to it.

Then I had the good sense to speak to my wife about my mad ideas and whilst she was all for it, she urged a little caution. She knew I could put my hand to a lot of idiotic things, but even though I played golf on the rare days I could get free, I had never actually built a golf course, and wouldn't it be a bright idea if I found someone who had done just that.

So I found John Lyons, or to be more accurate he found me, for I must have confided in someone that I was thinking seriously about building a golf course and the news spread.

John, who then had a handicap of about 4, wanted very much to find some land to exercise his skills. I had the land and we both found that we had a liking for Malt Whisky and we used to meet at the *Rising Sun*, run by a nice chap called Benstead and mentally pull my land apart to find the best area to build this golf course. Finally one evening, with a modicum of malt inside each of us and with the aid of the back of a packet of Players, we did in fact map out the present course.

Forty years or more ago a golf club used to consist of some hundred fanatical golfers, most of whom were City men, well trousered, who could afford the odd £40 to £50 which was the annual sub of that time. The course was looked after by at least 6 or 7 men who graduated from the farms and knew what a bit of good coloured grass was all about. They mowed the greens with machines that they pushed by hand and to get round the whole 18 greens often took them two days with four men doing the shoving.

The Club House was rough and not always ready but log fires and plenty of whisky kept the few members reasonably happy. The members were looked after by a man and his wife who generally lived in the village and more often than not had another part time job. When she had the time, the wife would often cook some home made cakes and on a week end there was generally a leg of lamb and a couple of veg for those members who were on the course for the day and didn't want to go back home. Drink was usually left out for the member to help himself and he always wrote down in the 'drinks book' what he had taken, for which he was billed at the end of the month or maybe the quarter.

The Secretary was definitely part time and generally turned up at the week end and only when the bar was manned, but to be fair to him, there wasn't a lot for him to do. There was no such thing then as the Monthly Medal, that was to come. However, there was the odd match either between members or even more rare, between other clubs and here of course the Secretary came into his own and checked what cards had been handed in and over further noggins, announced the winner for the day. He had some office work to do when the annual subs were due and very rarely he attended a committee meeting and took some notes which were never circulated and quite often were lost by the time the next yearly meeting occurred. But it didn't really matter, as everyone was frightfully matey and what someone had said a year ago, or thought they did, could always be said again.

The layout of the course evolved over the years by discussion between a few enthusiasts who took clubs onto a field, encouraged maybe by the owner of the field. Gradually the plan was worked out from tee to green, with various suggestions being made such as a bunker should go here, because old General Smith always bounced his drive about that spot and anyway his handicap was suspect and had been for years.

They were not interested in making a profit and they were not all that concerned if they made a loss for the year. The hon treasurer would get up at the AGM, which was well attended if a dozen or so turned up, and would say that we really ought to find a few hundred here and there and members would take their cheque books out and in minutes the small red figures would turn black — it was all so nice and leisurely, and very different to the rat race it is becoming today.

As a Secretary and owner of a golf club and one who travels round other clubs the whole set up is becoming more and more of a rat race and you cannot help but wonder how things are going to turn out.

When we started building this course life was fairly easy but most interesting for, members were pouring in, even before we had laid a green.

Before we could start making the greens we had to decide whether to use turf or sow grass seed. Various bowling clubs were visited and their grass inspected but we thought that we might do better and made enquiries to Wimbledon Tennis Club to ask where they got their grass when they wanted to relay a worn patch.

I should mention that I had married into a very famous tennis family for my wife's aunt, who went by the name of Aunt Chatty, actually won the Ladies Championship five times on a trot. The story was told that Chatty was bicycling home one day after having won Wimbledon when she saw her brother clipping his garden hedge, so when he called out and asked what she had been up to that afternoon she replied that she had just won Wimbledon "Oh good show," remarked her brother and went on clipping.

The main reason I wanted turf was because if we used seed it would take several years before a fourteen stone man could tread on it, whilst turf could be used within six months, so turf we got and John Lyons laid out all the greens, using planks for his men to tread on.

I had by now some hundred trusting members and some of them used to come up each weekend to see how we were getting on. About fifty of these kind people had attended the first meeting that I held down in the village hall in Otford, the object of this meeting was to assess how much support there would be for a new golf course in the area.

I confess I wondered whether anyone would turn up although I had inserted various advertisements in local papers and I got my accountant and solicitor to come and hold my hand, so to speak, the former to answer any questions on the cash side and my solicitor to deal with matters legal.

I was pretty certain that at least six men would turn up, for it was they who used to come along and knock on my back door when I was still farming and ask if they could hit a ball about in one of my fields. I always used to let them, but was careful to tell them whether 'Churchill' was about. Churchill was an Angus bull we had before we went over to AI. As an Angus he had no horns, but like most of his breed was intensely curious about anything that to him seemed somewhat odd. The sight of humans, with a sort of a stick hitting a little white ball hither and yon needed to be investigated at great speed, and one Sunday, one of the golfers came tearing back and said that my bull had gone berserk and would I do something about it — *now*.

I went along and had a look and there was Churchill stamping with fury on a perfectly innocent set of golf clubs. The owner had, with some dexterity, leaped the nearest fence and was looking somewhat sadly at a set of woods and irons which had been his pride and joy.

With some low cunning, I induced a bulling heifer to enter the field, which persuaded Churchill to stop destroying the set of clubs together with the bag and turn his thoughts to the production of cross bred beef calves.

We had arranged loads of chairs facing the platform in the village hall with little hope of filling any of them and I then took my two paid professionals next door to the village pub to imbibe some Dutch courage, but before we had time to down more than a pint, someone came in and asked when we were going to start as the hall was packed and had I any more chairs?

So back we went and there was the astonishing sight of a packed hall filled with serious looking men and even a few ladies could be seen, and so we took our seats in a cloud of beer fumes and tried to look respectable. After all, some of these men might have cheque books at the ready and all they wanted was the right sort of talk from me and their pens would come out as well.

So I heaved myself to my feet and started to unclutter what was in my mind. I told them that years ago my farm had been a famous course, opened by Henry Cotten, that the original club house was on offer to me and that I thought that there should be another course in the area if only to reduce the waiting lists on the existing ones. I told them that there was not a sign of the old course, except for the first hole but I intended to provide, with their backing, an interesting if not daunting 18 holes plus perhaps an extra 9, together with a five acre practice ground and sat down with my heart going pitter-patter. I then asked my solicitor to say a few words and then my accountant, and then we waited, for either everyone to get up and leave forthwith or show some interest, and interest there was in vast quantities. The questions came thick and fast — things that I had never thought about. Committees — how many? Would there be a Professional? What would be my role? Would I have a Secretary? What about the rough — would it be playable or 'lost ball stuff'?

This went on for about an hour and I thought that we had had enough, so stood up and asked for a show of hands that *if* I built a golf course they would back me. I really felt embarrassed for there was a roar of approval, hands shot in the air, cheque books were waved and I started to feel somewhat guilty for I was in the middle of combining the harvest. Although I was dammed certain that I was going to build the best course I could, it was going to take time and just hoped these kind people didn't think that in a week or two they would be playing golf on my course.

And it was about then that John Lyons and I got together. He had been at the meeting, he wanted to build a golf course and he came up and introduced himself.

My first paid up member was a nice man to whom I regret to say I was very rude, for he came waving a cheque book, and treading through my un-combined barley to which I had quite fortuitously undersown some quite good grass seed. Farmers tend to get a bit touchy when harvest time approaches. They have ploughed, disced and harrowed the fields and quite often rolled them; applied top dressing and of course sowed them with costly dressed seed and now watch the harvest grow and ripen. Sometimes twice a day the ears will be tested to see if the crop is ready.

The day comes when it is all go, the sun is shining, the drier is ready, the baler is ready, the combine is filled to the brim with fuel and off you go, the steady roar of the engine is like music to your ears, even better, looking behind you at the corn tank, you see the steady stream of cereal pouring in. Nothing but nothing must stop you now. You *MUST* finish this field by nightfall.

And then, striding through *YOUR* corn as if he owned it came a figure waving a bit of paper. He flattens this bit and then that bit, he has big feet and you have to stop — the last thing you want to do. I looked at this chap, and if looks could kill he would have died on the spot. I opened my mouth to yell at him above the roar of the combine engine but by this time he was flattening another bit of corn right by my side and I suddenly saw that the bit of paper was in fact a cheque and attached to the cheque was the new entry form for the Members to sign and send in with their money. I hastily altered my expression from one of utter fury to one of complete delight, was able to thank him above the roar of the engine and off he went, treading on more corn and I let in the clutch in a much happier mood, — we were in the golfing business.

I came to an agreement with the owners of the old club house and they departed leaving the place in a somewhat peculiar state. The old locker rooms were still in being and so were the lockers but I opened one and then another and out fell old tins and used cartons. The last owners had not felt it necessary to have the dustman call every week, for some reason best known to themselves and when they had a bit of rubbish to throw away, they found it easier to open an empty locker and throw the rubbish inside and quickly shut the door. They had been doing this for years.

I then had to take the decision to sell the cows and of course get out of milk deliveries to all my nice housewives, which was a bit of a wrench for they were responsible for a lot of income, not only milk, but eggs, farmyard manure, wood, and dogs, but cows and golfers would not mix. The mere thought of building quite a costly green and then having a herd of cows stroll across it, gave me sleepless nights, so the cows went and sold quite well and the money came in handy for paying for the old club house which needed central heating together with a few other things that had to be done to it.

Quite a bit later the sheep and lambs went, although I did have a couple of hundred ewes on the place when we finally opened it for play, and they only went because, quite simply, their manure. The ewes and their lambs found that bunkers were an ideal spot in which to sleep the night through. The sand was warm and what wind there might be, whistled over the top of the bunker, but ewes are lazy beasts; when they want to empty their bowels they merely grunt and out it comes, where they are lying at the time — in my bunkers. Next morning, before the staff had got around some golfing member would drive his nice clean white ball into a bunker, which was full of droppings, so there were complaints, not only for lost balls but having to play out of such a mess, so the sheep went and peace reigned. This was a pity because a sheep is one of the best machines made to convert tough old cocksfoot into pliable grass, still there it was, they went.

But I had not the slightest regret in getting rid of the cows for it was too much to be constructing a golf course and producing a thousand pints per day and delivering it to the back door/front door/dog kennel/shove it in the fridge love, so I was really relieved when the last pint went.

Although it was a toss up as to whether one was glad to see the back of the cows or the housewives, the former were time consuming and just a few of the latter were downright impossible, for she has this thought in her head that unless her milk is boiled, fried or generally fiddled about with, she will loose every baby she is carrying, her nails will drop off and her hair will become peculiar.

The dogs on the other hand were quite a money spinner because their owners never dreamt that I as a farmer knew anything about feeding animals and so they would give me half a dozen tins of dog food for little fido for him/her to eat.

Although we finished with delivering milk to all and sundry, we still used to get the odd call from an ex customer for some wood or manure. I used to say that I would only deliver by the trailer load as the mere thought of firstly finding suitable bags and then filling them was not just on. With a trailer it was simple, we merely attached the foreloading fork to the tractor and dug it into a heap of manure which Feckless, Heckless, etc., gave one without a further thought, quite often when you were pulling a pint from her. Loaded the trailer with about four good forkfuls and off we went. It was a bit awkward one particular day when I was trundling my somewhat smelly load towards a customer's house and called in to see where they wanted some two tons to be tipped. The man of the house indicated where, and I backed to the desired spot, lifted up the hydraulic lever and up the trailer went and tipped the lot over the family pram. More by luck than any judgement, the child had been taken in to have its rear end cleaned and washed. They were good customers, so I bought them another pram.

* * *

When the greens were all laid, the bunkers dug and sand off loaded into them, between each green and a nicely raised tee there was a blank of nothing, just the remains of the stubble from the harvest and here and there a little grass where I had undersown. So how to produce fairways and for that matter rough and semi rough? It seemed to me as a farmer of quite a few years standing that if I had the courage to do nothing, just damn all, and wait for the natural grasses to grow, with the assistance of a spot of fertiliser, I would have natural fairways, albeit with a modicum of weed which, if attacked with a mower, would soon give up the ghost and depart. And this is what we did; the natural grasses grew; we rolled them; they grew more and we snipped them here and there. We started to mark out fairways, always trying hard to make an interesting hole. We allowed the semi rough to grow up just a bit and the rough even more, but bearing in mind that we wanted a course where it was possible to find a ball if one was foolish enough to hit it off the fairways and not waste too much time trying to find it. I always thought that *if* you went into the rough then it was your own fault and you should be penalised, not by losing a ball but by having to take a wedge or similar to get back onto the fairway.

So roughly six months after that brave chap strode through my uncut barley we invited a few members to play just nine holes, for that was all we had ready for them and I must say they were more than happy with what they played on. We had been fortunate enough to be able to build some really formidable par 3's, one of which measured some 245 yards from tee to pin and I offered a prize of £100 to anyone out of the original 24 players who played and opened the course who could sink their put in par. Nobody, I am glad to say, was able to achieve that feat, for it was a drive across a shallow valley to a green perched aloft, and although in latter years we had some six players who did achieve their par, it was a tricky par 3.

When we opened the first nine holes the greens were more than rough and there were tramlines all over the place, but slowly they knitted together and in the end really made fine greens.

When we were renovating the old club house we took trailer loads of old tins and junk out of the place, and were amazed how they cooked for there was a very ancient electric cooker and alongside it was a pair of somewhat smelly gum boots. We soon found out why the gum boots were there for the stove was faintly live, and unless you wanted a severe shock you earthed yourself by wearing the boots. We put in sufficient radiators and an enormous iron wood stove in the bar room, for we had some 12 acres of wood and why not use it. We also heated the radiators with a vast boiler which would take, oil, wood, even a bale of straw.

I had a Dobermann at the time and he had fun dealing with the rats because the place was infested with them. How the last owners had lived with these sometimes vast creatures, I shall never know, but in the end we got rid of the lot.

We went to the local market and bought a number of arm chairs none of which I paid more that a fiver for, although by the time that one had put new covers on and they looked respectable, the cost had risen somewhat. I got hold of a brewer who installed beer, pumps and optics and a trifle reluctantly, glasses.

Finally I obtained a club licence from the Bench at Dartford, a one armed bandit and two full sized billiard tables, one of which, I again obtained at market for the vast sum of £50. As our membership had now had risen to some 200 souls I advised them that we would be opening on a certain date and at a certain time, and that drinks would be *free* for just one hour.

I must pay tribute to those early members who were so kind to me and were more than willing to paint, construct three bars — which we did all on our own — put up picture rails on which to hang future medal boards, and even got cracking on a garden round their future golf club house.

I had then to start thinking about committees and all that, and whereas I was more than willing for the members to have as many committees as they wanted, all minutes must come through my office for my signature before they were valid. One or two cliques made noises off stage because they thought the place was now a member's club and my wife and I were somewhat in the way, so I drew up a set of rules that I made everyone sign and out of the original 200, I had one resignation, which wasn't bad.

I had thought that I was fairly busy before all this golf caper started but as my shepherd had departed at more or less the same time as the sheep and of course my cowman had gone also with the last of the cows, I found myself, as the course was growing all on my little own but was saved by the presence of Albert.

Albert was 65, or so he said, could have been more, but he used to be employed at odd times during my farming years and he rang me up and said that he had heard that I was in the middle of this golf business and did I want a hand?

Too right I said, you can do from 06.00 to 12.00 from Monday to Saturday. "Doing what?" asked Albert, "caning the greens and raking the bunkers plus cleaning machinery," I replied.

And so for some three years give or take a month or two, that was how we started. Albert would stalk round all the greens, he was very tall and somewhat stately, carrying his cane in his hand, mounted on our motorized bunker raker and by 08.00 all were done.

Albert would then return and change 'steeds' to a small motorized grass cutter and he would wander round all the tees, both male and female, put the tee pegs either back or forward one exact foot and mow the whole 36.

The rest of his morning was spent in cleaning machinery, oil changing and all that sort of thing.

I did the rest on my little own. It sounds extraordinary to the modern golf course with at least six men on their pay roll, one wonders as to what they all do?

I had thought that I was fairly busy before all this golf caper started but now found myself doing the bar, the greens and quite often the fairways into the bargain. My wife, bless her, would do the breakfasts, and we had a nice soul who came from the village to sort out what was needed in the way of lunch, and my wife and I would turn our collective hands to what dinners were needed in the evening. I found myself drinking far too much, for everyone who came to the bar insisted that I had a drink with them and finally had to go over to the old dodge of making up a bottle of coloured water that looked like Scotch but wasn't. I always felt guilty at charging a member for my drink which really cost nothing.

I was then faced with the fact that although the course was coming on apace and the last nine would soon be ready, I only had one man to help me and time was becoming a bit critical, especially as the dry weather was coming on and the greens wanted a continuous supply of water. Although I had miles of hose pipe and sprinklers galore, there was a snag. Sometimes, when a golfer came to a green which was being carefully watered with the sprinkler whirling around it was in the way of their approach shot, so one of them would come along and move it but would quite forget to put it back. When I arrived at a given time on my little Honda motorcycle pursued now by a Great Dane and the rat catching Dobermann, I would find a dry green and a couple of bunkers in which you could breed trout. To overcome this snag I decided to get hold of a firm who would lay on underground pipes, place four, sometimes five pop-up sprinklers round a green and a few on each tee for good measure — the cost of this little exercise — £12,000. When that was done I took miles of hose pipe down to the local market and sold the lot, but what I had forgotten was that the spikes of golfers who had not taken the trouble to step *over* a hose pipe, pierced the hose in a number of places and I did get a few complaints.

Our watering system was a trifle Heath Robinson because I inherited a fairly deep bore right outside my back door, some 240 feet deep and with about 30 feet of water in it at all time; sometimes a bit more in the winter. I had, during my farming days, obtained a licence to abstract water, which seemed silly at the time, because although we owned the land and, of course, the water that fell on it, God help us if we took a pint out of this bore hole without permission.

But now it seemed silly not to incorporate it into the system for watering the greens as each green during the summer months wanted about an inch of water per week, and this was free. As it was a chalk bore I thought that I had better see whether the fissures of the chalk wanted cleaning out and poured down it a load of sulphuric acid and stood back as the fumes that poured out were somewhat bad for one's health.

But my 30 feet of water had risen to about 38 feet and to this I added all the water from the gutters off our old manor house and then set up a system of pumping that worked quite well over the years. I sank a pipe nearly to the bottom of the bore with an underwater pump attached and then lowered two wires, one negative and one positive, attached of course to the motor of the pump and switched on and up the water came, but when the level of the water reached the other wire, it stopped. It then went to another underground tank of huge proportions into which the end of the watering system was inserted. I added a time switch and kept my fingers crossed. It did work, and at about 04.00 every morning in the summer one green after another came into action which was fine except for the very early golfer who, on more than one occasion, would, whilst addressing his put be attacked from the rear by a jet of water at a considerable amount of pounds per square inch.

Explanations into the weekly news sheet that I had started some while ago were necessary, and was kept in the club house and to my surprise was read avidly by most of the members, spelling mistakes that I made (and still do) were neatly circled and great interest was shown as to who had done what, how and when. I used to insert bar prices for pubs in the area and then highlight ours to show that members were not being done over their beer and spirits.

On the subject of early golfers, I used to make it my practice to go round the course on the faithful Honda, together with the Dane and the Dobermann to do nothing else than catch the odd non paying golfer who had sneaked in for a free round. I confess that I quite often enjoyed these early morning forays, for the excuses that the foreign golfer gave would have filled a smallish book from, "Didn't think you had to pay till you finished the round, Guv", or "I always pay at the end of the week", or "I thought that it was free golf," and so on. I had a set drill for these occasions. I sat the Dobermann on one side of this would-be thief and the Dane on the other and told them both in plain English, "do not bite yet". Then demanded double the green fee, and generally got it.

Sometimes on these early morning forays I would inspect the watered greens and if I was not certain if the sprinklers had covered all the green I would buy about a gallon of red dye and insert it in the holding tank, and next morning there would be 18 red greens. If there was a streak of green, then all I had to do was to alter the sprinkler head a degree or two and that was that. But my office was then besieged by worried members who thought we had a horrid disease over all the greens and some of the tees and wanted to know what I was going to do about it.

For good measure I also put an ordinary rain gauge on a green to see what water was in it when I passed by the next morning and by this method I had a reasonable idea of the amount of water the greens were getting.

By this time I had some 500 members and my costs had risen to £24,000, i.e., £6,000 for the building of the course, turves and all that, £12,000 for the sprinkler system and last, but not least, £4,000 for the old club house.

Of course we had a few complaints, but nothing serious and I think we pleased some 80% of our membership, although there were always complainers, like the chap who would come into the office and complain that the loo paper was too hard or sometimes too soft. Then there was the bar staff. Again some member would complain that the pretty one behind the bar had spurned his well intentioned advances and didn't I think that I ought to tell her off, to which I replied that he should know better at his age and with a nice wife and family to boot. When I next saw the 'pretty one', I gave her a quid, and said swiftly that there were no strings attached.

I only once had a crooked member of staff and she didn't really work in the bar. She was a cleaner, and she used to hoover around the place most mornings. After wandering round the course I would come in and undo the alarm and let her in and then check the bar takings for the previous day, enter it all up into a book, and take out of store a spare bottle of this and that to last through that particular day. I had installed a somewhat complicated bar till which, when you pressed the right button would ring up a scotch or a gin or a beer or any system of nine numbers and so I could check the measures left in the bottles. Once a week I would be missing a whole new bottle of whisky, and for the life of me I could not see what was going wrong because I trusted the bar staff. After she had finished, my cleaning lady used to take my Hoover back to her house for she thought it might get pinched if she left it at the club, and also I suspect that she used it on her own house. So what? thought I, she was welcome. But one morning I was walking, for a change, and she and I met in the middle of the road. I said, "Good Morning," and she put my Hoover down, for it must have been a bit heavy for her and there was a faint clinking sound of glass on the road surface — and the penny dropped. I opened the bag on the Hoover and there, nestling amongst the rubbish, was a full bottle of *my* whisky. We parted, she and I, then and there.

I was serving drinks to four green fee players on one occasion, and as they had no idea who I was, their remarks were most interesting.

According to them the course was the most interesting they had played on for quite a while They thought that the top half was a bit tight, and I silently agreed with them for there were three holes in which you could not afford to slice or pull a shot, but they waxed ecstatic over the first and the ninth and two of them thought that they might apply for membership. "Any idea what the owner is like," asked one? "Lucky bastard," replied his mate, "doing nothing all day bar swing a golf club," and then that 'pretty little thing' came into the bar to take over from me and called me "Sir". There was a faint 'ush' from the other side of the bar and I got out quickly, but I heard one ask my nice wee thing, "Who was that?" "The Boss man," I heard her say.

One trouble on the course was flints. Bloody great things that poked their 'snouts' through the fairways and I had to do something about them otherwise there would be a lot of complaints, so I bought a large four ton roller, which the tractors could just about pull, and that settled the hash of the flints. Of course, in time, the compacting of the soil by the continued use of the roller got my drainage all in a pickle, so once again I had to go out and buy a large machine with a lot of spikes attached to it, and that made nice holes all over the place so that the surface water could drain away.

Peace then reigned for a while, for by now Albert had retired and I had two men on the course, plus myself, and we could mow the greens in three hours flat, or I could, because I did tend to pull a bit of rank when I was mowing a green. I took a dim view of any golfer who yelled at me to get out of the way, and some words were exchanged at times.

Another essential job was the caning of the greens every morning to get the dew off them, for dew and golf greens don't always mix. Disease comes along and one has trouble, so this was quite often included in my early morning rounds with the two dogs, and whilst I was at it, I shifted the tee boxes on both the men and ladies' tees, a yard a day. I found that worked quite well.

One of the many mistakes that we made when we built the course was to make all the tees far to small; they got worn out in weeks, so I got out my faithful old bull-dozer and made 36 new tees — 18 for the men and 18 for the ladies— all of the size of a cricket pitch and about 11 feet wide with small slopes, so that when I was doing the fairways I could also run over all the tees with the hydraulic mowers. I always cut the fairways and the rough for the first few weeks of the season. I disliked straight holes, and decided they should be made interesting, and to a certain extent, the more dog legs the better. I also liked to have semi rough next door to the actual fairway — round about 12 feet of it for the mowers. Mounted on a tractor were six mowers which would cut just that amount and it was simple to raise them half an inch, so as to create the semi rough.

The rough itself is a subject open to argument all over the golfing world, as it depends really who owns the course. If the members own the place then of course they can have rough ten feet high if they wish. It's their patch and they can do what they want. In this case it was a bit different as I owned the place and I was dependent to a certain extent on the cash brought in by green fee visitors and at that time it was in the region of £45,000 per annum.

The average visitor merely wants a spot of fairly cheap exercise chasing a white ball round a few miles of nicely mown grass. If he makes a muck up of his drive (after all, quite a few of us do just that) he doesn't want to spend hours looking for it, for the five minute rule is unknown to him. What is more important, he wants to finish his round in three hours and a bit, get back into the club house with his mates, have a jar or three, some quick cooked nice food and be back in the working rat race which he avoided with possibly some guile that very morning. So the rough must be of a texture to penalise the golfer if he gets into it, but he must be able to find the ball in quick time — if he doesn't then he will never come near this course again.

Visitors were welcome on five days of the week but the week-ends belonged to the members and them alone and the car parks would often be full by 09.00, a lot of them having started at 05.00 or before. We tried various formats of playing. Two players and two balls, three players and three balls, four players and four balls and even four players with two balls, but the consensus of opinion was that the first option was by far the best. We also tried ball shoots and finally we stuck to starting sheets at 8 minute intervals. It was also important that starting sheets went up at exactly the same time on the same day, and I did this myself at 06.00 prompt every three weeks on a Sunday morning. I spent hours of hard earned time taking phone calls from members who wanted their names put down on a certain day and for a certain time, and even went to the trouble of buying myself a mobile phone that I could take round the house. I well remember one day when I was enthroned in one of our smallish rooms attending to the needs of nature with the phone stuck in my pocket, and it rang. The member on the other end was most insistent that I drop anything that I was doing (I had done just that from the trouser point of view) and *rush*, not proceed, but actually rush to the starting sheets and insert his name for 08.00 the following Saturday, because he happened to know that another member, who he disliked, wanted that time and none other. That was the straw that broke my more than usually willing back, and I told the chap concerned exactly where I was and that if he was really all that keen, he could drive up and do it himself, or ring the Pro's shop, but I was going to continue sitting where I was for a while.

I should have mentioned my excellent Golf Professionals. The man concerned was Ken Adwick, who was a tower of strength and a nice chap to work with, but I didn't actually start with him. I was about to start with someone else, and to show what little I knew in the early days about running a golf course, I had no idea that a Golf Pro' would demand a thing called a retainer. He would not be content to take the profit from selling his golf ware out of a rent free, heat free, and sometimes phone free shop, plus of course the fees that he would get from members or others who wanted lessons, but he had to have this retainer. So when I first met this chap, it was he who asked me if I wanted a Pro, and I seem to remember saying something to the effect that I might as well, why not? But that evening the phone went and a voice said that he was the agent or manager of this Pro and could he have my cheque for £1,000 forthwith and then the contract would be drawn up. Not on your nelly, said I, so that was that, till Ken Adwick came along and we did come to terms that suited both of us. He got a cut from the green fees, his shop was rent free and I supplied the wood for his wood burning stove and Ken used to go away on cruises and teach golf on board some super liner, whilst his assistant held the fort.

It was about this time that I started the *Shotgun Sunday do* which we held about twice during the summer months and the only way I knew when we could get 72 players back off the course all more or less at the same time. It went like this. Firstly we put up a list asking for players with a limit of 72, then the draw was made to see who was playing with who, but the actual format was fourball and in the draw it was also decided where each fourball would start. Say the fourball drew tee No 3, OK, and finished on Green 2 and their *combined* score, less the correct handicaps for each player would be handed in to the Secretary. The previous evening there was an *Auction Dinner* which cost each player £10, for which he got a decent three course dinner and some wine thrown in for good measure. Bets were placed by members on who would come home with the best score (net) and I gave the winning team £100 to be divided up between them. It was a great success all round, the Club made something out of it, the members had a great day and after the first *Shotgun* the lists were always oversubscribed. The only thing that I had to remember, amongst a few other trifles, was that Honda and I, plus of course dogs, and me armed with my 12 bore would have to be at the highest part of the course and at exactly the right time, to fire both barrels which was the signal for 72 players to drive off.

Round about our second year, I started the *Golfing Ladder* which proved to be popular and this was simply several long boards with slots cut into the wood about an inch apart at an angle and each slot contained the name and phone number of a Member. If your name was below, say Smith, you phoned Smith and challenged him to a match over in this case, nine holes, and Smith had to accept the challenge within a certain time, three days I think was the norm, you gave Smith 50p and you gave the Secretary(which at that time also happened to be me) another 50p. If you beat Smith, then your name moved up one and you challenged the next card above your name or Smith might challenge you again, but on Christmas day I would present the name at the top of the heap with the sum of £300, I made some money, the members made some money but the main thing was that everyone got to know everyone else.

Fathers were then started, which was simply a means of looking after a new member and seeing that he was never left on his own to mooch around. He always had his 'Father' who would introduce him to other members. If a new member was introduced by an existing member then that was easy, the existing member became the 'Father' figure and showed the newcomer what to do and in some case what *not* to do.

A Member's Club is different in that a new member *has* to be introduced by an existing member, but an Owners Club differs in that a man or woman can come along to my office, on the rare occasion when I am able to find the time to be in it and ask me the simple question whether he or she can become a member. I used to adopt a sort of dialogue. Why did they want to join with us? Had they been a member of another club, and if so, where? What handicap had they and how far away did they live? I would then thank them for coming and give some excuse or other and say that I would let them know in a day or two as to whether we would be able to fit them in.

If they had been a member of another club, I would ring the Secretary — all Secretaries of golf clubs are quite close knit — and when I had made my number, I would ask him about this chap who says that he was a member with you, what was he like?

If the answer was that his 'maths' were a bit dicey (which meant that his score card was peculiar) or something even worse, then I sent a letter to the person concerned saying that we were full to the brim with members of his particular handicap. But if he or she were nice, looked as if they got on with people of all sorts and types, then he or she could write a cheque out then and there and I would find them a 'Father', or in the case of a lady, a 'Mother'. But whereas it was easy to find a suitable willing 'Father', I always had some slight trouble with our worthy ladies. I had the feeling that if some female wanted to belong to this club then let her get on with it.

One of my next problems was the question of new members who had never played the game before but wanted to join a golf club in order to learn, which was fair enough, but I couldn't metaphorically, after taking their well earned boodle, throw them onto a golf course, more or less naked, without being taught something. So I used to say to these worthy people, OK, we will take you on but you are *not* allowed onto the course till you have filled in a suitable card on our beginner's course and you are in the Pro's hands. This gave Ken Adwick a bit of extra cash and we planned out a three holer which the budding beginner had to go round in a certain score. Then and only then, would he or she be allowed out with the big boys.

So we came into our third or fourth year when, in one of our annual get-togethers of Secretaries of golf courses, I was asked when I was going to get myself a Secretary. So I put the word out, and here of course I was a fool. I thought that a Secretary would be able to do everything that I did, from mowing the greens, doing the fairways, tidying up a bunker, caning a green, serving out a pint, to cooking a steak and chips. You name it, or think of it, I did it. A chap phoned and his references were so perfect that I took him on there and then, never having seen him. How idiotic could one get?

One weekend he arrived in a Rolls together with his cat, and its bag of fish. Even I could hear that the Rolls was missing on one cylinder, and I was somewhat confused when, taking him to task about its missing cylinder, he remarked, "Dear Boy, I am uncertain as to how to open the bonnet."

He made it plain, even before he opened the door of this five cylinder Rolls that I was on trial, not he, his work would consist of merely a weekend, that he expected a room in my house for that period and that my garden should be free of dogs so that he could exercise his cat.

When I foolishly mentioned the question of mowing the greens at the weekend when the staff were normally off duty and I was on, he mentioned that he had often wanted to see this done, but as he slept in for the morning so as not to disturb the cat, he hadn't a clue. Perhaps I could arrange a demonstration at say about 11.00 hrs., always providing the weather was fine and the sun was shining, and he would be delighted to come and watch.

I stood all this for about two weeks and then decided that he was not really my cup of tea. My wife felt the same for the curtains of his room were torn to shreds by the dear cat and he had the habit of opening his window, which was on the third floor, and emptying the 'presents' of the cat over the window of my sister-in-law who slept below him. During this time I had mended the sixth cylinder and he departed, without regrets on either side, but the Rolls purred and so maybe did the cat.

My next venture into obtaining a Secretary was a lot better and a more delightful chap you would be hard put to find. He was an ex Squadron Leader in the RAF and had been a Secretary of a south coast club for quite a while but was intrigued to find a golf club actually owned by one man where he would not be ruled by a Committee. Which, by the way, was the main reason why he left his last club.

But he had nowhere to live so we bought him a house down in Otford, our nearest village where, for a while, he and his wife seemed to be happy, but it soon became clear that this nice chap had a drink problem, his wife stopped liking him and she departed. After a while so did he, but in the year or so that I had the pleasure of his company life for both of us was more than pleasant.

Then, nothing daunted, I met and liked a man called Adrian Boler who was a Secretary to a famous Club near us and he liked the idea of not having a committee telling him what to do. In fact as my second in command he could tell the various committees what he wanted *them* to do, so I had the great pleasure of working with him for some three years or more with never even a written agreement between us. Adrian died of cancer and I was with him on the day before he died. I told him silly tales about members of the club who we both knew and at rare times there was a ghost of a smile on his thin gaunt features for he had been unable to eat for at least a week. He died the next day and I wept for him and his nice wife for our mutual friendship was something very rare between two men, especially if one was in theory if not in fact, his Boss.

Whilst Adrian was in charge I had the chance to make some extra money out of the club and the first means was with my boat. I have always been keen on 'mucking about' in boats and the one I had then was a Nicholson 38 Ketch which I kept down at Brighton Marina. I put up a notice on the club board that I was willing to take up to four members for the day, either fishing or I would teach them something about sailing and if they were really interested, then navigation together with Sat-Nav would be on the Agenda. I was over subscribed from day one and I would take parties of four, with some food and drink as well, provide the necessary transport and take them back to their various homes in the evening They were willing to pay quite a bit which helped a lot towards the mooring fees down at the Marina.

Then came fly fishing, which started when I found a place on the course where the ground was always wet, so I took a dowsing stick and found that there was a spring quite close to the surface. I got my old tractor with a front fork and soon dug a small lake which made that particular golf hole a lot more interesting, but it also made an area on which one could cast a fly. Soon members were wanting to learn this not so easy sport, so more vital cash came in.

Then there was photography. I had a camera which would take a series of shots and tried this out on Adrian. I found that 8 or nine shots with a golf club hitting a ball would quite often show up a fault in the swing, or the feet, or the head if they were all put together one after the other, so a bit more cash came in.

Also I started to teach some of the members of the green committee what work was all about on a golf course. After all, I argued, if you, as a committee, tell the head greensman to do some task (through me) then would it not be a good idea if you actually could do the job yourself. It goes without saying that I did not charge anything for this.

Shooting was another money spinner, and I ran shooting lessons with a 12 bore although not a lot of members were interested but again it brought in some much needed extra cash.

Some of the bigger houses in the district had substantial lawns, and cutting these was also very lucrative, for I would run the Toro (Greens mower) up onto a trailer and take it to the lawn in question and as the Toro made a six foot cut, it was short work to do number of lawns, and the owners of these lawns liked to tell their friends that their lawns had been cut by professionals from the local golf club.

Snow fell and our small lanes were blocked solid, so I asked the Council whether they would like me to clear them. "What with," they asked. "My bulldozer," I replied. To which laconic conversation I added, "How much are you prepared to pay me?" They mentioned a figure that was so far in advance to what I used to get contract ploughing or combining, that I accepted right away.

There is a limit to the amount of snow that can be pushed so I angled the blade to make a bank of snow to the left, and then to the right on the return journey. This effectively sealed the drives and entrances of every house in the two miles or more that I cleared — there must have been at least twenty — and I imprisoned the lot. Their cars, wives and children who should have been taken to school and, of course, even more important, the husbands who wanted to motor down to the local railway station.

I knew most of them quite well — in fact some were members of my golf club — and some of them found that the easiest way to get their respective drives unblocked was to wave a bottle of Scotch at me as I slowly chugged past on my clanking treads. I would then swiftly pull the correct track lever, lumber round, clear a path for the householder concerned, have sippers on the way and then move onto the next snowed up dwelling. I confess to having been more than happy that no police car was able to get up to our hills.

I was approached by a group of about a dozen men who wanted to know whether I would be willing to have an artisan membership. In those days, not so much now, an artisan golfer was a man who belonged to a club but because he was generally asked to pay very little for his membership, he was expected to do some unpaid work round the course. "What," I asked, "are you prepared to do round the course?" Some said early morning bunkers, which was fine, others said that they would keep the gardens round the club house tidy, which would be handy and so we came to an agreement. They could use the 19th as their own but, of course, the member could also use it; they would do *all* the bunkers on a Sunday morning and on Saturday the garden team must do the garden and for that I would charge them half a five-day membership fee and they could play three times per week but must start off before 07.00. This scheme worked quite well for a number of years, till first one then another moved away and finally it died a natural death.

One thing I learnt fairly early on in my new profession is that your greens staff *must* be able to play golf and if possible be reasonably good at it. It stands to reason that if they don't play the game then they are apt to do stupid things which will annoy members. Also I was able to introduce teams of green-keepers to play all round the county on other courses free of green fees. This proved to be more than beneficial to the club on whose course the match was about to be played for I noticed that although the place generally looked good, on those days the place seemed to glisten.

'The Captain's table', as it was called, was formed by past captains with the main idea not only to have a yearly dinner, but to get the captain elect to propose to the other captains who he would like to have as his running mate. Generally whoever was chosen was unanimously elected, for after all the captain-to-be had to work and depend on the man concerned. We did the voting on the old black ball principal, which meant all the captains had one white ball and one black ball and so, for that matter, did I. And if *one* black ball was found in the box concerned, then we all had to think again, but of course nobody knew who had placed a black ball in the box which saved a lot of bother. I never charged the captain for the year a subscription as I reckoned it cost him quite a bit of money out of his own pocket, and he was also helping the club which meant in some ways, myself. The captain always had the choice of times on the starting sheets and generally he and the Pro would take on any other challenging pair every Sunday morning, and he, like me, would sit on all Committees.

By 1973 we were almost full to the brim, I had put a ceiling of

500 seven-day members, 250 five-day members and 100 juniors, plus, of course, the ladies section which had about 250 full members and a number of week-day ones. The associate members, i.e., those who wanted to join, had no handicap but were trying hard to obtain one, numbered, at that time, in the region of 45, and they kept the Pro's shop more than busy with their lessons out on the practice grounds and in the nets.

There was a moment of near panic at the end of the year when a new motorway was proposed which would have cut the whole place in half, and having served on the council for a couple of years, I was able in a small way to point out the snags of that particular route to all and sundry and I was more than thankful that somebody must have listened for the idea was shelved.

The holiday camp almost next door to us, the first one ever formed as far as I know and to whom I used to deliver a whole churn full of milk every day during the season, decided to close down and I bought one of their cottages which gave us three tied houses. Also I was fortunate enough to be able to employ Syd. He was our first handyman. He was never late and was never ill. He could do more or less anything that needed doing and if he couldn't do a job then he soon found out how. As long as he was not asked to sit on a tractor or have anything to do with the actual running of the golf course, then from brick-laying, to plumbing, to electrical work, to plastering, Syd was our man.

The beginning of 1975 brought in the voucher system, disliked by at least 20% of our members, but as far as I could judge — and the committees were behind me — it had to come if the members wanted a club house fully manned from morning to night, where they could get a drink more or less at anytime, a full blown meal into the bargain, a warm atmosphere, a game of snooker, even to watching a large TV one had to have staff and staff cost money. I suppose all this started because of *boot members*. These were members who came somewhat furtively into the car park dressed as city men, opened the car door, threw off city wear, donned golfing garments and sped off and did their 18 holes and came back, repeated the clothes business and off they went, never subscribing a single penny to the upkeep of the club house. So having warned members what to expect I stuck £50 on each sub in the form of vouchers which they could exchange for food or drink or anything that we sold in the three bars, but no change would be given, i.e., you could not buy a box of matches, present a £1.00 voucher and get change. About twenty members wrote furious letters and resigned, three of whom I happen to know joined other clubs who put £100 as vouchers onto their next sub — the biter was bit.

On the other hand at least 4% of the members never bothered to bring their voucher books along to the bar and therefore paid the full price for their beer and food.

About this time my son, Richard joined us and he ran the club house, was responsible for catering and manned the bar to boot and life for me changed a lot for the better. It was so nice having my own son actually working *with* me and of course the lad had done his cookery course. Suddenly the members understood that they were getting really well cooked grub and not stuff that I used to throw at them from time to time.

Bingley arrived to do their yearly inspection — not only of us — but hundreds of other courses round the South of England; well worth the money to have experts crawl round the place, examine every known weed and pronounce what I should do about it, and I used to publish their findings in the weekly news sheet, which at times gave me quite a lot of pleasure.

Now that I had Adrian Boler firmly in the saddle, we found, to our delight, that we could actually afford the time to take a holiday and we decided that we would fly to the sun — Barbados in fact. This would be the first time that I had flown since 1941 when, as a very young 2nd Lieut. in the ack-ack, I had been ordered by a kind Brigadier to go and have a look at the German flak and see if they were any good. The reasoning behind the Brigadier's mind was that I found myself teaching this very senior officer how to use, of all things, a 12 bore shot gun. For once a month — assuming that we had the time — the Regiment used to set up a trap shoot and having used a 12 bore since a child, I found it was reasonably easy. The Brigadier, who took part in this exercise, found it was quite impossible and asked my CO who this youngster was who kept on shooting these clays out of the sky. When I was presented, somewhat sheepishly, to my Brigadier I had to explain to him, as if to a child, that if you put the target in the middle of an imaginary clock face and shot up on the line of the minute hand, more often than not you would hit the target. The Brigadier tried this and after a while he also found that it worked, which brought us to the question of using this principal over open sights on, say a 40 mm Bofors. "My Troop have been doing just that for months, Sir," I piped up. "Who taught them?" asked this now quite interested senior officer. "Me, Sir," said I, wondering whether I was doing something quite utterly wrong. "I am sending you on a course, Leet," says the Brig. and off I went to become a sort of instructor of gunnery and in the middle of this course I was told about the German flak and ordered to report my findings.

I reported to an aerodrome on the east coast and one fine evening found myself speeding down the runway on board a two engined bomber. Over the North Sea we flew and on our arrival off the enemy coast the crew had orders to throw out loads of leaflets, which as far as I remember advised the Germans to surrender at once if not sooner. Their immediate answer to this was to open up with every anti aircraft gun they had and the sky was suddenly alight with all sorts of coloured missiles and several of these hit our plane killing two of the crew and what was just as unpleasant, one of our engines was knocked out. Our pilot took a dim view of all this and turned round and headed back across the now very cold looking North Sea loosing height as we went.

This young pilot had the habit of speaking his innermost thoughts out aloud, and he didn't improve matters by repeating every few minutes that he really couldn't see how we were going to make it. But we did, just, and found at the last moment that we had no undercarriage and landed somewhat brokenly in a field and he and I found ourselves the only live persons to stagger off this wreck. I reported back to my Brigadier that in my considered opinion, the German flak was excellent.

I repeated this exercise in a four engined bomber which was just that slightly bit worse in that two engines were knocked out and limping home on the return journey, the pilot suggested to the remaining three of the crew — the others were dead — that as he thought they were over land, they could, if they so wished, jump for it. His reasoning was that he knew that he would have to make a belly landing on two engines and he didn't think much of our chances, so gave us the choice. I chose to remain, as the very thought of heaving myself out into the blackness made me feel worse than I was. The others jumped and were never seen again for I think the pilot was wrong, and we were over the sea. Anyway we landed, once again in a ploughed field, and we walked away from the wreckage of what was, several hours ago, quite a pleasant looking aircraft.

And now, having avoided flying for years, once again I was going to fly, and I cannot say I enjoyed the flight and the landing was more than unpleasant, but only in my mind. But the sun was wonderful after dull and wet England and we returned just in time to 'Shoot in' the new captain

This was quite a day in the life of the club and members turned up in their droves to see the captain make a balls up of his first drive off the tee. It appeared to be the done thing to try and put the poor chap off with a lot of shouting and, of course, I was there with the trusty 12 bore and the idea was that I should fire it as he actually hit the ball. We did have a captain who got so nervous about the whole thing that he missed the ball altogether, and another time some member changed the captain's ball for one made of chocolate and he ended up somewhat messy.

After he had traditionally driven himself into the job, we all trooped back to the club house and the new captain stood everyone a drink and that was that, a taxi was generally called, for the new captain was in no fit state to drive.

THE FIRE

Things were going well, membership was about full, the club house was popular and generally quite crowded up to 21.00 hrs when we shut shop. The one armed bandit was going berserk and societies were enjoying us. In fact one society enjoyed themselves to such an extent that one of them forgot to extinguish his cigarette and left it in an armchair and the whole club house went up in flames.

Not that it really adds to this story, but I have always liked to sleep in the nude and I was awakened at about 02.00 by the hooting of a horn outside our window.

Leaping out of bed without a thought I drew back the curtains and looked straight into the eyes of the wife of the bar steward who lived in a flat by the side of the club house. Modestly averting her eyes she yelled from the car for me to ring the fire brigade as the club house was well alight.

By the time I had found my teeth and crammed them in, found a pair of trousers for the bottom half and a sweater for the top, the first fire appliance — I am told that one must no longer call them fire engines — was sweeping into the car park, and timing its arrival as the roof of our old club house caved in with a roar. Two more fire appliances arrived but the first snag in all this furore was when the first appliance ran out of water and the head man wanted to know where the fire hydrant happened to be situated. Having lived in the place for the best part of 27 years I felt a bit of a twit as I shouted above the roar of the fire that I was sorry, but I had not the slightest idea.

Then I got one of my brilliant ideas — at the time it seemed so — and pointed to a manhole cover in the car park and asked the fire people to open it up and they would find thousands of gallons of water down there for all the water from the adjacent roofs ran into this enormous underground tank. A lot of fire hoses snaked their way down into the depths and water shot out and started to dowse the flames, but I had forgotten one little fact. The underground tank also took all the slurry from the cow shed, now part of the Pro's shop, and very soon first one hose and then another started to falter and the jet of water became a dribble and finally stopped. Every hose was jammed solid with slurry and the stench was past believing for if you throw liquid manure into a blazing fire, it does pong, to say the least. The firemen were not all that much amused at the thought that every one of their pumps was now solid with you know what, but the fire was out, although there was nothing left of what had been a nice old-fashioned club house in which hundreds of people had enjoyed themselves, day after day and night after night for years.

At this stage, it must have been about 03.00 hrs, two past captains who lived near at hand appeared on the scene and we found ourselves in the middle of a car park, smelly to the extreme, holding what must have been an extra ordinary committee meeting, of which no minutes were taken. By 05.00 hrs it was all over, the smouldering embers were quiet and the fire chaps had taken to making a cup of tea and I departed, after thanking them for their efforts and passed round a bottle of Scotch to temper their tea just a little.

Back to the house for an early cooked breakfast only to be called to the phone half way through eating a sausage by a man who called himself a fire assessor who said that I should do *nothing* till he and I had a chat. I went back to my sausage only to hear the back door bell pealing and there was another man, who was also a fire assessor, trying to get in but was blocked my Hamish, my Dane, who took a dim view of strangers coming through the back door without the boss letting them in. Disentangled Hamish from this man's trousers, not without some effort, which didn't do the trousers much good and once again went back to my now, coldish sausage. Went down to the sodden and blackened car park to find not one but *three* fire assessors regarding each other with a baleful eye and was able to carry out a sort of Dutch auction, first going to one for his lowest quote and then trotting over to the next and asking him whether he could beat that, and in this fashion I was able to save myself some £2,000.

I then rang up my brewers and explained the situation and asked them for glasses, beer, tables and anything else that they could give me, for I aimed to turn an old barn of ours into a temporary club house and open *that very evening.*

The brewers were not interested, so I told them what they could do with their beer and then rang up a family firm of brewers in Kent, who promised that everything would be delivered *that morning.*

I took all the men — now three — off the course, explained that I wanted at least twenty young trees cut down, gave them the measurements, and yelled for Syd telling him what I wanted him to do. Then I sat down at the phone and got hold of my insurance company. Having the OK from them I got four builders to come along *now* to give me a quote for a new club house. That was the morning gone.

During the afternoon the trees were brought down from the wood and laid across a ledge on either side of the old barn so making a false ceiling, and we found some stack netting to drape over them. In the middle of all this the new brewers — bless them — turned up with everything, and I mean just that — everything. That evening we sold our first pint and a lot of spirits to an astonished group of members. We were back in business.

I went to bed that night worn to the marrow. The whole episode was not assisted by the vague thought in my mind that whereas I held a drinks licence for selling liquor in the old club house, I did not hold a licence to sell exactly the same material a few yards away in our old barn. Time will no doubt tell, I said to myself as I drifted off.

I then had to sort out the couple who had held the franchise for food and drink in the old club house. They took a somewhat dim view of their new surroundings compared to the old, and as it was not their fault, I took them on as wage earners till they could find themselves another job.

The fire taught me a number of things. I had forgotten to insure telephones, electric meters, the one armed bandit and the big one was the loss of profits. With hindsight it was a fool thing to open up the barn the same evening as the fire. My insurance company refused anything in the shape of profit loss because in their minds I merely carried on business, but the news had spread and that evening members turned up in their droves. The President came along for the ride, I was prodded into making a so-called speech, the President replied and altogether it was quite a night. My wife said that during my sleep I twitched from head to toe.

Our nice lady Captain came and saw me the next morning in my office and said that she wanted to ask me something. "Ah yes," I said, and waited. But nothing came. She obviously wanted something from me, or for me to do something. After a long pause I said, "Now what is it you want to talk about?" "Well," she said, and then in a rush, "is your lady secretary about"? "Next door," I said, and off she trotted to see my clever girl who coped with all my letters and generally kept the office turning over. The lady Captain left and my girl came in with a grin. "It's the question of a loo for the ladies, and the lady Captain felt a bit shy in asking you about such matters. She much admired the way you have created a new club house, but her ladies now have to walk some fifty yards, sometimes in dire urgency, in order to spend a penny."

We had a small hut of sorts which was situated on the high part of the course, where the wind, when it wanted to whine, really went to London Town, and members huddled in it, had a quick drag on a fag, decided that this was the spot where they wanted a new ball, so always dropped the wrapper on the floor. A courting couple were even found in the depths of winter with the lady looking discontented as the member in question, who must with deep regret remain nameless, had problems with the Arctic temperature and should really have come armed with a blow torch.

We took the hut to bits and rebuilt it next door to our new rustic club house and installed a thunder bin, bolted down onto sleepers — ladies for the use of.

Builders were asked to give estimates and the first one talked way over my financial head for we had some £65,000 to spend, plus a bit more for the contents, so I plied him with a gin and asked him to think again.

Syd was in his element with our new rustic club house and asked me if I thought we ought to have a fireplace in it. "Of course," said I, "can you build one?" "But of course, Guv. Now I shall want a brick or three," says our Syd. Bricks arrived the next morning and in two days time we had a massive fireplace which would take a two foot log. We purchased a large twelve foot metal pipe for the chimney, cut a hole in the roof and it went like a bomb. A week or two went by, we had settled with a builder, the site was cleared and material was coming in by the lorry load.

Now I have always got on well with our local bobby, a nice chap who lived in a village not far from us and liked his round of golf, which he rightly insisted on paying for, although at rare times he would imbibe a free pint of beer. I knew him in my farming days and was not too surprised when he called to see me and came straight to the point and said, "Are you aware, sir, that you are breaking the law by selling drink on these premises?"

"No," I said, "I have a licence from the Dartford Bench to do just that."

"In the old club house you had," said he.

"But it's only a few yards away," says I, in pleading note.
"Sorry, sir, but you are breaking the law."

"Would it be satisfactory from the point of view of the law if I gave the stuff away free?"

"Oh yes, sir, that would be within the law. There's nothing wrong in giving the stuff away."

So whilst he was in the bar, sipping an illegal pint of my beer, I wrote out a notice in large letters for all to see and it read like this.

THE DRINK IN THIS BAR IS FREE
but should you wish to give a donation to club funds then the following might suit your pocket *and* the Law.

After that I listed the bar prices.

"How's that," I asked my friendly policeman?

"Very neat, sir," and wished us well and he and his Panda departed.

I then contacted the Clerk of the Magistrates Court and asked when I could have a hearing to transfer my licence from the 'Ashes' to the barn.

The building of the new club house went on apace. The usual arguments took place such as when, for instance, I requested that the new building be built on the foundations of the old I found that the builders couldn't understand basic English. Thank goodness I was wide awake or I would have lost a foot all round — but it was going up, and that was what mattered.

We had lost so much of our memorabilia, like the Hole-in-one Board with the names of the members who were allowed to wear that particular tie. We even had a couple of King Holers marked up in gold letters. Gone too was The Lonely Hearts Board with all the names and phone numbers of people who wanted a game on a certain day, and other members would ring them and fix up a game — it was a popular idea.

And so one day, I paid out the final cheque and was given the keys. We said farewell to our old Barn with its false ceiling of tree trunks from the wood and the huge fireplace that Syd had created and entered somewhat cautiously into our new domain, all spotless, no smoky atmosphere and that evening the place was packed. We had sent round an invitation to all and sundry that from such and such a time the drinks would be on the new house, come along, bring your wife, and see what you have in the shape of a new club house.

After Adrian Boler died, I was lucky enough to obtain another Secretary who was a member of the club anyway, but before I took him on I told him that I wanted him to be able to do what I did if necessary. How to set a mower down to $^3/_{16}$ ths, how to mow a green, how to cut a fairway, change a hole, cut a hedge, and when he had mastered all that, I showed him round the innards of a bar, how to pull a pint, how to treat the customer, learn the art of making the member feel that he is wanted, be able to keep three bars going on his own, clean the beer pipes and so on. Finally I prodded our willing Pro' into taking him into his shop for a week to see what went on there behind the scenes.

Lastly he came to the office. This part was easier for he was a trained accountant and he was able to put my somewhat ancient book-keeping into a better state for all concerned. You see I have this somewhat odd (to some people) bee in my bonnet, that if you are going to manage something or somebody, you ought to be able to do their job as well as they can, but if possible, *better*, so that if perchance they do make a balls up you can show them how it should be done.

I gradually found that I was working myself out of a job. The Secretary was efficient, the staff appeared to be happy and even the club house staff appeared to be staying, for at the best of times they were apt to be somewhat nomadic and I must admit that I cannot say I blamed them. Boredom and long hours were coupled with the fact that some of our members were apt to treat them like dirt. I have at times been in the club house on my own, on the public side of the bar, drinking a reflective pint and a member would stride up to the bar, bang on the counter, and shout, 'PINT'. No 'Good morning'. No 'Please', and the very idea of saying 'Thank you' would never enter his head.

I would, if I was quick enough to catch the Steward's eye, shake my head, and the Steward would understand and drift off into the back quarters leaving the member standing puce with rage. I would then wander slowly round to the serving side myself and say, "Good morning, Mr Smith, why not try all that again." It would only take a few moments and I would, if I was feeling kindly, offer to pay for Smith's pint, but not often, and he would learn, our Mr Smith that nice saying, pertaining to a Wykehamist, that, 'Manners maketh man'. Who knows, it might even improve his golf, and if he wanted to resign then and there I would be only too delighted to assist him. But in the main, our members were a delight, to me anyway. One or two used to get on each other's nerves somewhat, like that nice couple who always booked the 09.00 slot every Monday. If it was raining then they came and played snooker, or if they were feeling very active they would hire badminton rackets and shuttlecocks and get a sweat up on the badminton court.

I was highly amused when a conversation overheard in the bar was reported to me verbatim between two golfers, alias Smith and Jones. They were discussing the reasons for slicing and hooking, and ways to overcome the problem. The question that Jones asked Smith was why, after taking a shot that wasn't dead straight, did Smith retire behind a bush for a short length of time, whilst Jones was doing his best to hit his ball straight.

The round would continue with Smith doing his disappearing act every now and then and Jones would get so curious that it would put him off his game, for he was convinced that the whole thing came down to gamesmanship and nothing else.

After the game, which as usual, Smith won easily, Jones handed over his £1. Filling his friend's glass for the second time, he felt he *must* ask Smith what he actually did behind the bushes.

Smith took his time in replying, and finishing his glass asked if he might have another whilst gathering his thoughts. When the next free full glass was put in front of him, he fixed his opponent with a mild but firm eye and asked him whether he purchased his golfing trousers off the peg or had them made for him. Jones answered that he generally had them made for him, to which Smith asked him if his tailor asked him the usual question as to whether he dressed to the left or right. Jones replied that his tailor did and that he dressed to the right.

"Ah," said Smith, "I knew you did."

"Why?" said Jones.

"Because you always slice," said Smith. "You see its all a question of balance; when I slice, being a modest man, I go behind a bush and adjust my dress for the next stoke."

I felt very flattered the other day when a green fee man came up to me and congratulated *me* on *his* lawn. "Let me explain," said this chap. "I buy your cores and have done for years, I suppose I must buy half a ton off you every year, put them through a sort of home made shredder and sprinkle the result over my lawn, and my goodness, it does grow; no wonder your greens are looking so well."

We always spiked our greens every year, and what is known as hollow tined them. This made about 100 3″ deep holes every square yard on the green. We then swept up the cores and whereas most golf courses threw them away, I thought it would be a good idea to bag them up and sell them to anyone who wanted a decent bit of soil, for a fair amount of fertiliser is placed on a green every year. In fact I used to send some cores to Bingley, they would send me back the soil content and I would place their findings on the bag. At a £1 per bag it was more than handy cash coming in throughout the growing season.

Found in the suggestion book the other day, written by a member with a vast lawn by the sound of it, 'What do you dress your greens with to make them look so much better than my lawn?'

Well now, if you really want to know, the following are the ingredients. Sulphate of ammonia, calcinated sulphate of iron, dried blood, powdered sulphate, bone meal, sulphate of potash, *and* if you are putting this on *dry*, then you want a base of peat, and mix the lot together. We used to do that but we found that if we left out the peat and mixed the remainder, shoved it all down into the holding tank from which we water the greens, then we were doing two jobs at the same time, i.e. watering the greens and applying the necessary fertiliser. I have not given you the quantities for one would want to see your lawn first, but that is the basic answer to your question.

Another suggestion written by a no doubt ill tempered member — and possibly worse for strong ale — was that he couldn't see why the club house always had to shut, just when he was getting into his stride, as he put it. The simple answer is for the members to take over the running of the club house, and to pay me a suitable rent.

Thank goodness we invested in more machinery than we really needed, for the other day I found that the head greenkeeper was on a well earned week's holiday, the second in command was in bed with flu and the junior was attending the birth of his first son. Fortunately I was able to cut all the fairways, the rough and the tees in five hours flat and, thanks to the kindness of some members, cut all the greens, including the winter ones, before the sun was even thinking of setting.

No doubt about it, the arrival of the new Ferguson 35, complete with seven hydraulically controlled two foot cutters, made a vast difference, and not only in the time taken to do a job. I enjoyed the ease of cutting the fairways down to one level, and then, by just raising the lot with one small finger to skim over the rough, and of course the tees, which I made with this in mind, so that again raising all seven cutters with this hard working single finger, each tee, measuring the length of a cricket pitch was done within one very small minute. This particular machine is so versatile that most of the sides and the backs of the bunkers can be done with one sweep, so 130 acres of golf course were done by one aged owner in just one day. I must admit that I did have a Scotch or three by the end of the evening.

It was about this time in the history of this little exploration of life that my wife and I decided that we would form a company and let it become a buffer 'twixt members and us. Members themselves were not all that happy about the situation for they kept on asking as to whom they might complain/ suggest/ congratulate, to which I was able to answer that I would pass their message on to the company, which of course was me, together with wife and children. But from the tax point of view, it was handy and should both of us run out of road or something similar then our offspring would be better off. Our AGMs were generally held whilst I was shaving and my wife was in the bath, which fact did not go down in the minutes.

On one of our yearly visits by Bingley, I was quite flattered when the inspector praised our winter greens, and as his visit was in the autumn his remarks were quite significant, for it might not be long before we played on them.

I have always had the idea that the winter play should be nearly as good as the summer, and that really meant the green, for that was where the scoring happened. So, in conjunction with my green committee I always marked out a spot quite early in the year, away from the main green as far as was practical, and treated it throughout the year *exactly* as a green. When the main green was spiked, the winter one was spiked and so on, the only thing that I had to contend with was the dear, dear member, who at the drop of a tee peg would trundle his heavy trolley across its surface and even, I hate to say, take a wedge off it. So I painted a white circle round each one and stuck up little notices such as G.U.R (ground under repair) and others that came to mind, anything to stop the wear and tear, so that when winter really set in, the members would have something decent on which to putt. Bingley liked the idea, and various Secretaries from near by clubs used to drop in, not only for a beer and a chat but to see our winter greens.

I liked the idea of keeping the Members informed as to whether we made a loss or a profit and in the early days after the whole course had been completed and there was only Albert, aged 65 and me aged then about 45, running the place, we did in the second year, creep out of the red figures into the black, a mere thousand or two *BUT* a profit nevertheless.

In our best year, a figure never to be repeated, we did reach the giddy heights of £42,678 net into my ex-farming plebian pocket, but as I explained to a somewhat disbelieving load of Secretaries at one of our yearly meetings, this figure would be impossible to achieve in a Members Club.

WHY? Because of Committees and the impossibility of getting a 'gaggle' of disinterested people to agree about anything that they knew nothing about.

Take the average Golf Club Green Committee, they are all or were experts in their own field, they knew next to nothing about grass land management which is what a Golf Club is all about (or nearly so).

But with me and others of the same ilk who were ex-farmers and who ran their own show, life was reasonably simple. If you, for instance found your fairways a bit 'skint' of grass, you applied top dressing. If you found moss in vast quantities, then you applied lime. You didn't have to ask countless very nice Members as to whether you were allowed to, you got on and did it.

And then from my point of view, that quite reasonably nice profit was not all achieved with anything to do with golf at all. There was the boat. That, in itself made quite a nice profit with Members coming down for a weekend afloat. There was a host of other 'things' such as the mowing of private lawns. That in itself was around about £4,000. The one-armed bandit, merely because I obtained a 'machine' that paid out £200 for the insertion of a mere 10p. That raised at least £12,000 and there were countless other 'exercises' that the Members appeared to like, which all contributed to the a/m net profit, *BUT* I repeat, a Members Club run by the Members could never do it. You have to have one man at the helm, trusted by all.

I liked the idea of keeping the members informed how our finances were performing, for after all it was partly due to him or her that we made any profit at all. This particular year, as far as my plebeian mind could see, we had made £18,760 profit after most of the costs had been paid, although to keep the possibly jealous member at bay as to why I may have earned all that, I added that that particular sum could at any moment be swallowed up by the purchase of a new machine.

I have the idea that some of them thought that I got up, had my breakfast at about 10.00, read the paper for an hour, ambled down to the office to make the time of day with my efficient secretary, and then galloped to the club house for the first gin and tonic of the day. Let me set that little idea correct for starters. During the summer I would be off by 05.30 a.m. on my little Honda, pursued by the two dogs, to 'do' the course, and on my journey, intercepting the odd very early golfer who hadn't paid his green fee, and then to the golf club and to the bar, but not to imbibe, merely to do the accounts via the optics and the till of yesterday's takings. By then there would be the odd player who would like a green fee ticket and that money would also go into the till. Then the one armed bandit which at that time I owned and I would undo its backsides and withdraw what money it had abstracted from the box concerned and again that would go down into the bar till. By this time, the staff would have appeared, having clocked in and we would have a chat as to what wanted doing.

Then back to breakfast and the mail, which I would deal with whilst munching a decent breakfast made by my long suffering but rather nice wife. To deal with the mail, I would natter into a tape recorder whilst attacking the breakfast and would then depart to the office and present the tape to my efficient secretary. I might then have to interview a possible new member or deal with such similar items for an hour and then at about 11.00 I would mount a tractor and deal with some job that at our earlier meeting with the staff, I had arranged to do.

At 12.00 I would be on hand for the daily surgery, sometimes held in the bar, at other times held in my office. This was all member's stuff, complaints would come from some earnest type that as he had piles, could we have a softer type of loo paper, to another chap who liked to read his daily newspaper in the locker room after having a shower and would it possible to *reduce* the heat of the hot water for he was nearly scalded the other day. Then at around about 13.00 I would return to the house with both dogs to heel and partake of lunch, watched by a Dane on one side and a Dobermann on the other, and if I was fool enough to give one a morsel and was a bit slower with the other's gift all hell would break loose. At 14.00 I would be back on a tractor doing something on the course, or up in the woods, again with a tractor and trailer but now armed with a chain saw for the club house needed a never ending supply of logs measuring round about 3 feet in length. I would pack it in at tea time, have a cuppa and maybe if there was a committee meeting on I would attend it, and finally supper and to bed.

Once a year all the golf club Secretaries gather at a golf club where they pay for their drink and food but the course is free and in the afternoon numerous four balls show each other how they think that the game is played. But before all that happens, there is a meeting and as there are no club members present, hair is let down so to speak, and Secretaries speak their mind on how ghastly their particular committees are in general and some of their own members in particular. I should have pointed out that when I got the notice of this meeting, where it will take place, the date and the time, there may be a footnote saying that I would be expected to say a few words and I would be asked to explain why I, a mere ex-farmer who had the gall to own a golf course and had had a hand in making it, should make so much more profit than most of them. Profit is probably the wrong word for out of the hundred or so Secretaries who used to turn up to these meetings, at least half or possibly more admitted that they actually made a loss and would increase their annual subs to take care of the situation. I should also have mentioned that out of the clubs that were represented there were at least a dozen privately owned ones such as mine and we *all* made a profit, and when my name was called and I lumbered to my feet full of decent beer, I pointed out that I was possibly unique in that some of my profit was made from *boats*, teaching fly fishing, and of course mowing the squire's lawns, and of all things, the selling of cores off the greens at £1 per bag; which took some swallowing from the representatives of member's clubs. The voucher system came in for quite a bit of stick from my fellow Secretaries, whose committees forbade the mere mention of the word in their own hallowed halls, but most of the owner's clubs went in for it and it *worked*.

Members occasionally asked why we displayed a list of lapsed subscriptions. The reason was that the club's licence was issued strictly on the understanding that alcohol could *only* be served to members, and if they had not paid their subs they couldn't be served, for they were no longer members.

The other reason was that the member who looks after handicaps wants to know whether a name *should* be on the list or not. Again, if you have not paid, then you are no longer a member and therefore have no handicap in the club. There is nearly always a waiting list of people wanting membership, and if you are no longer a member, then your slot can be filled by somebody else.

My son Richard who had been in charge of the bar and the catering decided that he really *must* find a job on his own and in due course he purchased the Rose and Crown in Mayfield, Sussex and after two years working with me, he and his family departed, which was a blow for it is very nice to be part and parcel of a family business as this was, but progress must go on so off they went and another couple took over the Franchise of the bar and the catering.

About this time, a man called and for some reason wanted to buy Matilda. She, if you remember, was a crawler tractor which did yeoman work constructing the course and also, when she was in the mood, pulled a six furrow 9″ plough. This, of course, when I was farming.

The price was right, so I said farewell to her and bought myself (with your money, I hasten to add) a JCB. That is a 'thing' closely aligned to a tractor but with a vast bucket looking affair out in front and with which, so the smart looking salesman assured me, I would be able, under his tuition, to pick an egg off the deck after a few hours. He was right; in fact half an hour was enough. The egg, plus a bit of earth, was safely in the bucket.

We are now once again in search of an experienced tractor driver. The vacancy occurred because one of our nice bunch decided that he would be better off in Australia than here, and with my good wishes and some well earned advice from me, off he and his family departed.

I have now seen some 18 would be experts, most of whom were much more interested in the rent free house and the better by far wage than the farming one, but the trouble was that most if not all had not the slightest idea how to start a tractor let alone drive the thing.

I got a long form filled out and dug down to see, or tried to see, whether the man concerned had ever worked on a farm at all. I got excited with one who actually appeared to know quite a bit about tractors, he even knew that a diesel tractor doesn't have plugs, only to find, after some half a dozen phone calls that he was a washer of tractors, but had never actually driven one.

Five out of the 18 could actually start the engine but were quite flummoxed when I stuck a trailer on the rear end and invited them to back it through a gate. Tricky in some of our narrow lanes with a ruddy great lorry approaching in a hurry.

So I am down to three and have decided that John Friend, our head green-keeper can decide. After all, it is he who has to work with the chap.

I am asked by a keen Member who is a Farmer some 60 miles

away as to my running costs per year — who knows he also might
want to start a golf course — so for his use and maybe your interest:

1969 – £ 7,316	1972 – £25,534
1970 – £15,106	1973 – £31,624
1971 – £19,403	1974 – £42,131

I wish I had a crystal ball to tell me what 1975 will bring forth,
leaving out the question of new staff and their salary which is a
known factor, but how much will oil cost, from about 7p in 1969 to
over 20p in 1974. Fertiliser from £16 per ton to over £80 today,
grass seed, the good stuff such as Pencross from under £100 per ton
to £485 today.

I had one of those interesting complaints the other day. By
interesting, I mean not the ordinary run-of-the-mill complaints which
generally dealt with such mundane subjects as *loo paper*, it was
either too soft or too hard , or the beer was far too dear, or the
course, in particular the par 3s were far too tricky. No, this was
interesting because it dealt with human excreta — put in its politest
manner that I can think of. This chap was complaining that although
he *saw* the tees being cut early that morning, when he came to play
at about 12.00, there were inch long *weeds* growing which put him
off.

He was even more annoyed when I suggested that he could have
as many as he could pull up without making ruddy great holes all
over the place. "What are they?" he asked.

"Tomato plants," I replied.

And then all this business about the tons of *black stuff* that the
members would see arriving, had to be explained. You see ever since
we started this golfing lark I had been buying in loads of this
material from the local sewerage farm run by the Council. The cost
of it was very cheap, in fact I feel that the Council was glad to be rid
of it, but from my point of view, it was cheaper by far than top soil,
and also more important, it had a fair amount of goodness in it BUT
it also had thousands upon thousands of tomato seeds, which the
human stomach cannot destroy and nor could the sewerage farms,
thus the ever growing plants on most of the tees.

TIED HOUSES

Often the centre of controversy. From the point of view of the worker, not all that bad, always providing that you can get on with the Boss man, and also that if the wife wants something done in the house concerned, then the Boss will do it, and not forgetting that the worker concerned is living rent and rates free. *But*, on the other hand, again from the worker's point of view, if you give your notice in, or God forbid, you get the sack you have a month in which to get yourself and your family out of the house. From the side of the owner, you have a man, one of your team, more or less on your doorstep and although you pay his rates and he lives rent free, it is not a bad situation, always providing that the man concerned does not become — a squatter.

This is what happened to us. The man concerned got fed up with golf courses and wanted to return to good honest ploughing and gave me notice. I advertised for another man, and when I found him, after some trials and tribulations, I told him that the post *and* the house was his with effect from a certain date, which was a week *after* the present man *should* have quit my cottage *but he didn't*.

To make matters even worse, my new man had given notice to *his* employer that he would be leaving his tied cottage on a certain date, but he couldn't because his future home was being squatted in.

So I had to go to court and request an eviction order which was granted in a *month*'s time which meant that my new man, if he was going to be correct *should* have left his tied cottage.

What a mess. I was assisted by a good neighbour who owed me a favour or three and who just happened to have a vacant cottage and my new man and his long suffering wife moved in whilst waiting for my eviction order to be executed.

Just for the record Sunday Lunch, February 7th 1976. Roast Beef and two veg. - 50p.

HOLE-IN-ONE

No doubt about it, but we do have some interesting par 3s and having in the early days been a bit more of a twit than usual, I made it plain that I would present any member in a *Competition* with the not so small sum of £25 *if* he or she would do just that, and marked of course by their opponent.

Those of you who know the course will remember the Eiger (No.1) with either hate or horror but it is the first par 3 and one could say that it is quite steep, a mere one in four, and it had never, up to March 6th, been conquered till Mr J.F.S., stepped on to the tee and 'batting' with a four wood, sank the ball into the hole. But not to be outdone by this achievement, the very next day Mr M.S. did the very same thing, but this time with a two iron. A costly 48 hours.

LAWNS — PRIVATE FOR THE USE OF

Members keep on asking what they should put on their lawns and having produced this bit of information some while ago *but* in liquid form, here is what I feel (and Bingly agrees) is what your lawn should have 'thrown' at it in the late spring. In powder *but* water it in well and do not tread on it for at least three days. Per 100 square yards you want. 28 lbs sandy compost, 1 lb sulphate of potash, 1 lb fine bone meal, 5 lbs of powdered super phosphate, 2 lbs dried blood, 3 lbs sulphate of ammonia.

Having put it on, with a bit of luck a small garden spreader, do the spreading in your golf shoes with decent spikes on them, it helps.

Lastly with private lawns, don't be tempted to mow *below* $^5/_{16}$ of an inch till the end of May. Whilst you are at it, don't guess what $^5/_{16}$ of an inch might look like, do the job properly. Turn your mower upside down, after removing what petrol you might have had left in your tank (it is probably stale anyway), then get a straight edge and place it from the front roller to the back one and the distance between your sole plate and your straight edge should be $^5/_{16}$. If not, adjust, using some oil if you find the job difficult, the adjusting screws will thank you.

Whilst you have your mower in this interesting position you might as well align the blades, they cut better if you do.

Cut yourself a bit of firm paper, say about an inch wide and six inches long (don't forget to remove the plug lead, fingers are irreplaceable) and place the paper on the sole plate, then turn the blades by hand and the paper should cut in the same way all along the sole plate. If it doesn't there are two more locking nuts that you have forgotten to lubricate during the winter.

The new one armed bandit, now paying out a £200 jackpot is popular with one member — he took his wife for a weekend in Paris — it cost him 10p.

Generally in a club of any sort, there is always someone who takes a dim view of someone else. Are you with me? In this case I was the 'someone else' and whenever I met this chap, he always blamed me for something or other. If he had had a bad round, I was to blame. There was nothing as far as he was concerned that I did right, so I was somewhat amused to hear from our head green-keeper, who was acting barman one evening, that having served Mr X with a pint, he leaned over the bar and in a very confidential manner, as if he didn't want anyone else to hear, started to praise the efforts of the head green-keeper on the state of the fairways and how clever he had been in shaping them and not having long straight lines as some other clubs do.

At the end of this eulogy the head green-keeper thanked the member very much but couldn't resist saying that he wasn't responsible for the fairways, it was the 'Guv' who always did this particular job.

Mr X is alleged to have put down his half finished pint and walked off without a word. I, on the other hand, having suffered at the hands of this gentleman for some considerable time could not resist penning him a line, thanking him for his praise and popped it into his pigeon hole. He never spoke to me again.

Once again the daunting prospect looms that yet once again we shall have to engage new bar and catering staff. If you as a member here are not certain of this particular picture, let me try and put you in the 'frame' so to speak.

Since my son left to earn his living in a pub of his own, you, the member have suffered the attentions, however well meaning of various stewards and their families. You had the nice husband and a wife, whose look, if it was her bad day, would strike you dead. You had the charming wife and the husband who thought that the world in general and you, the member, owed them a living and a damn good one at that. And then not forgetting the couple who could never for some odd reason best known to themselves, give you the right change and they loved the idea that if you paid for a double, you actually got a single *and* the wrong change.

So now we are going to try a well known catering firm who will charge us for their expertise to the tune of £3,000 per annum plus of course I have to pay their wages and they get a small amount of the profits (if any).

The situation would be better if we could rid ourselves of our 'boot' members, those nice chaps who arrive and scuttle out of their driving seats into the boot and in a flash appear as a golfer and reverse the procedure in three hours' time. He doesn't even spend a penny in the club house, he does that around about the 16th where the bushes are dying for some reason or other!

Lastly, and I will leave the club house alone for a while, a member asked as to what it costs to run the place for a week. The answer is no change out of £350.00.

But if this last scheme doesn't work then vouchers, willy-nilly, will come into their own.

Congratulations to our tallest member who was the top of the ladder on Christmas Day and I sent him a cheque for £300 as was usual. Now we have the 'chore' of extracting all the names off the 'ladder', mixing them all up and getting our Junior Captain to pick out card after card so that we can start again. If you were near the top of the 'heap' and now you find yourself near the bottom, see the Junior Captain, not me.

We started something new in the golf world the other day (1977) and it went like this. Members would come and see me and say that they have friends who would love to join a private golf club but the trouble is that they are unable to raise enough 'boodle' to put down £200 in one fell swoop. This sum includes entrance, annual sub, VAT, E.G.U etc. So we have arranged that providing the applicant is, shall we say, suitable *and* can qualify from the playing angle, then he or she can pay by direct debit, say once per quarter. This proved quite popular and once again we are full to the brim with 500 seven-day members, 50 six-day members, and 200 five-day members.

Once again the club house has changed, the catering firm has gone, far too costly from my point of view and now we have the place run by a couple on a franchise and wonder upon wonder, they actually pay *me* a modicum.

The course continues to be looked after by just two excellent men, helped now and then by me. In fact you could say that I do most, if not all, of the fairways and most of the rough and I am about to lessen the work load and do away with the Ladies' Tees and put our worthy lady members on the front of the men's tees, for after all the men's tees are 22 yards long and I am sure the LGU will take this in their stride.

Of course I could not do all this unless I had such an efficient Secretary who puts up with me and possibly you, the member and on the subject of members and the Secretary, the following might be apt.

Club Members to me,
I think you'll agree
Are as to a shepherd, his sheep,
I chase them off here
And pen them in there,
And count them, as I go to sleep.

As their eyes glisten,
I have to listen
To tales of marvellous putts
All I've seen them sink,
Is a great deal of drink
It's slowly driving me nuts.

They tell me with force,
What to do with the course
How drinks are cheaper in pubs
I'd like to suggest,
If ever pressed
Where they could place their clubs.

And when at last.
The ultimate blast,
Of the dear old trumpet calls,
They'll expect me to be,
On the fiery first tee,
With a box of asbestos balls!

DIARY OF RUNNING A GOLF COURSE

MARCH

I find that March is the time of the year, that if you are a dabbler, like me, in what I fondly call a veg patch, there is a tendency, unless I am more than wary, to get my proverbial knickers in a twist.

Problem is that you struggle through a foul February with a seed catalogue clutched in both work soiled hands and that you plant, sowing, everything that the catalogue allows both inside and out.

You keep glancing at the other pile that you tell yourself (Scouts honour and all that) that you mustn't even look at, let alone touch till the Ides of March were looming ahead.

But the weather is so kindly that I am well ahead of my chore of mowing the fairways on the golf course. I have done my morning 'surgery', and taken on a new member — a nice girl — and remind the lady captain that she might need 'mothering'.

Therefore, perhaps just a small look at the seed packets — no harm in that? The ground *is* so friable and I have had to take my coat off because it is more than warm, and before I could say, Carter's seeds, half a row of tomato seeds have gone in.

From one thing to another and still on things earthy, those of you who played golf today, I trust that you have looked at the half a dozen notices that strew your path to the first *and* the tenth tee. It says quite clearly, although possibly not in this fashion, DON'T LICK YOUR BALLS.

Now as to the reason behind this odd utterance. WORMS. Millions of them on your course. They pop up in the line of your putt, and they appear, sliding past your excellent lie on the fairway. Those of you who went and saw that nice play *Arsenic and Old Lace* will remember that arsenic plays merry hell with the human stomach. Worms are not all that keen on it either, which is why, when these creatures become a menace to all and sundry, we, the custodians of your golfing pleasure take steps to get rid of these creatures by spraying arsenic round the course, and your ball might just get attached to a wee bit, so do not, when you see a bit of dirt on your ball, lick it off.

This is also the time of year when you might find the head green-keeper or myself in a furtive sort of fashion taking cores from each green, popping them in a package, with the name of the green on them. These samples are then dried and a small portion is placed in a test tube, some liquid added, the whole thing shaken firmly and left to settle. After a time we look at the colour and we can tell whether we are all wrong with the following: lime, nitrogen and potash. Sometimes, I hasten to add, we find ourselves dead right and do not have to add anything to that particular green.

The list is up for those of you who want to come sailing and maybe, if you are interested, learn something about navigation and sorting out a Nicholson 38's three sails. We can if you wish, and the weather is reasonable, make a passage to the Sovereign Lighthouse — about five hours there and back. Bring your own grub, I will supply suitable 'hooch', the cost per person per trip – £15. Number of crew wanted, four. Wet gear is provided. Jerseys — bring your own.

Very rude of me, I forgot the wives. Last year and the year before, I was gently ticked off by a wife whose husband used to enjoy these day-long trips, who told his wife that females were not welcome. Not a word of truth in this. In fact if the ladies golf section want to 'fling' a foursome into this sailing business, you are more than welcome.

Maybe I should once again warn all of you who want to come this year that I carry out 'man overboard exercise' in quite a literal manner.

Next week I haul her out of the water and clean her 'bum' and apply antifoul so as to keep her weed free for the season. Actually all that happens is that we motor her to a couple of large posts on the high tide and wait for the water to leave her high and dry and then do the necessary work, before the tide comes in and floats her off.

We have a new gadget called Sat Nav which will give you her position anywhere in the Northern Area within roughly, 100 yards, the radar will show you France as soon as you are free from the harbour mouth and the RT (Radio Telephone) works well so that you can ring up your wife/husband when you are next door to the Sovereign.

And lastly if you want to fish, short rods and spinners only please.

We have a member who without a doubt is a keen gardener. He possibly might have a wife who doesn't like to see rubbish left about and our Syd whose many jobs include cleaning up our car parks every day is no longer amused, for this nice golfing/gardening member of ours cleans up his own garden every Saturday. That is the day he comes to us and plays a round and brings with him a nice large, quite clean, black bag, full of *his* garden rubbish. You know the sort of stuff I mean, weeds, dead plants and all that. And he tries to stuff it into *our* bins which we supply round all the car parks but the trouble is that it doesn't quite fit, so he plonks it on the ground next to said bin and departs to correct his slice.

Syd then comes along and clears up the sack and he has complained to me and now I, through the medium of this news sheet, would like to ask this nice tidy member of ours to stop bringing his rubbish to us — please!

SOCIETIES

Years ago we decided that for better or maybe worse, we would have to have Societies playing here, because for the simple reason that we needed the boodle. But we did view each one that arrived with some suspicion. What were they going to smash? What degree of rudeness would they display to the staff? Would we have any light bulbs left when they departed, and would members come screaming to the Secretary complaining about the 'six ball' in front of them who wouldn't give way for love or money?

Before I go on, my apologies to those Societies who are actually composed of human beings and are run well by their own Secretary.

But now after some years we have been quietly composing a black list of Societies that, come hell or high water, will never set foot on this turf again and that list is also, with others, taken up to the AGM of Golf Club Secretaries in the Southern Counties.

The other day we added yet another name to the growing list.

All Societies, when they book an available date with a golf club are sent a list of do's and don'ts and their Secretary concerned sends back a wee slip showing that he agrees with the terms set out, such as dress in the Club House and other quite normal regulations.

So when I rolled down to the Club House, after a hard day at 18.15 hrs., I was interested in observing a sort of figure reclining in one of our arm chairs in the lounge. He was slowly but with great thoroughness, picking his nose with a very dirty prehensile finger nail that had, with some inborn skill, been fashioned for that particular job. He was in a sweat shirt that had a lot of visible sweat attached to it and whether it had ever had the pleasure of viewing the inside of a washing machine, remained a question. One armpit had a large hole in it, through which dangled a large mass of reddish coloured hair. The result of the nose excavations were being placed with some care underneath one of our better armchairs.

Glancing with growing anger at the rest of this interesting torso, from his face that hadn't seen a razor blade for at least three days, to his fly buttons which were undone and to his feet which were lacking shoes, but clinging to them were some very smelly socks, suitably decorated with various holes, through which peeped toenails that were jet black.

I found the Secretary of this Society and took him gently by the arm and showed him this interesting specimen of *homo sapiens*, to which he gave me one of those looks which said that he had done his best, but couldn't do more.

So I went to the owner of the filthy toenails, and quickly lifting his glass, remarked that he would find it in the 19th, unless I spilt it on the way.

His language was ripe but I was considerably bigger than he and he came quietly muttering.

Now that is yet another Society which just might find it hard to obtain another booking in the south of England.

APRIL

It now being April, I am afraid that this is the time when some 800 envelopes are licked and our franking machine goes berserk and the end result spoils your breakfast in a few days time. Annual subs are due. The first home run is as usual for the last eleven years, rewarded with a bottle of Scotch, and just as a matter of interest, according to my records, this bottle has been won by the same man for three years running.

From one thing to another, I must get down to thanking our nice Captain for presenting me with the Leet shield with the Leet Arms all blazing away. But I will try and satisfy some of the queries as to what the thing is all about.

It all started a while ago with or maybe without the blessing of Mother Church in 1085, give or take a day or so. When a Thane of King Edward the Confessor, decided that some Thanes should be called 'Leit'. This name once started changed now and then to Lete, Leyt, Let, Lyte till round about 1566, a chap called LEET got fed up with spelling his name any old way and settled down in Cambridge with the firm intention to breed as fast as he, and for good measure, his wife, could make it.

Going back to the Crest itself, one has to drift back in time to the Holy Wars of the Crusaders where the Thanes (or Lets) of England supported their King in the capture of Jerusalem from those nasty heathen, the Muhammadans.

The dress for battle in those days consisted of anything that was heavy enough to resist a sword cut or thrust and was bloody hot in the midday Syrian sun, so the Knights in their somewhat sweaty chain mail devised what came to be known as a sur-coat. A light garment that deflected the rays of the sun. That was fine and everyone was a bit cooler but everyone looked alike and dear old Edward didn't know who was who, so the Knights emblazoned their sur-coats with their family 'mark' and the one hanging nicely on the lounge wall happened to belong to my family. The two lighted coils denoted that the bearer had been in the Holy Wars for they were a favourite weapon of the Turks who, dipping a bit of rope into some black stuff which oozed out of the ground, (we now call it oil) lit it and flung it smartly twixt the feet of the galloping horses of the a/m Lets (Thanes), which caused some mayhem, one way and another. The ducal coronet denoted command and the bird concerned was a Martlet.

So Mr Captain on behalf of all the Leits, Lytes, Leets, thank you very much.

I am asked, in fact it is more like a demand, from a lady member here who decided that she also would like to come sailing, to explain how a ship's loo works. Firstly dear lady, not that it matters a hoot but people who muck about in boats, call what you call a loo, a head. But not to worry.

There is without a doubt a certain difference between a land or shore based loo to a sea-going, head. So when I am confronted in the middle of the ocean by a cross legged female who wants to 'go' I start like this.

Now first turn that big 'gate valve'. "What is a gate valve?" asks cross-legs, so I show her for the second time. Turn this thing, so that the handle faces forward towards the sharp end of the boat, that we call the bow. "Oh blast the bow," says she, "Get on with it." Then put your hand *under* the pan and search for the valve and turn it *on* (to the left) I added for good measure. When you have finished what you came in for, pump with that lever, so that your 'offering' goes out to the fishes and then control the amount of sea water coming *in* with that little silver valve, then finally turn off the gate valve and leave the handle facing aft.

What I never tell them on any account that if perchance they are actually enthroned and the boat drops smartly off a twenty foot wave the surge effect in the pan should be felt to be believed.

Lastly on the subject of 'heads' I used to put a little notice up which read. "Nothing down here you ain't ate", providing my crew could read, it saved a lot of bother.

Having dealt with the transom end of my female crew it is only proper for the Skipper to try and deal with the possible 'Cordonbleumanship' of the lady in question, if you don't you will find strings of onions tied round your binoculars, minced beef in the chain locker, and when you break the spinnaker out, fresh vegetables will flutter all over the deck.

Try the old adage, 'Tin to Tum' it's a lot simpler. Although we did have one lady crew a while ago who, brainy girl that she was, found that most boats carry a bit of cool bilge water and we were no exception. The trouble with that idea is that after 24 hours, every label has been washed off.

There are continual rumours floating about that I and my family are about to sell the place and go and bask in the sun somewhere for the autumn of our lives.

Just let me say this on that subject. If, just *if* some idiot came along and offered me a stupid high price, then who knows I might just accept and I would get out of the hot seat once and for all. I have in truth had one or two offers, but I can assure you that *if* we ever decided to get serious about this matter, I would of course be duty bound to offer it, the whole shooting match, i.e., one seven bedroomed Manor House, three cottages, a Club House, a Pro's shop and various barns, an 18 hole Golf Course and another 100 acres or so, plus about £50,000 worth of machinery, to those nice people, my Members.

I have no idea where this selling business started, certainly not from me for although I started on a shoestring and for a while my near farming overdraft became a certain golf one and my meagre black figures turned smartly to red more or less overnight but during the last few years things have improved no end and in fact, although I should not probably mention it, I did in fact buy some long term gilts the other day.

But this so-called prosperity has not relied solely on golf, the boat for instance covers its costs easily and in the last few years has shown a decent profit. The mowing of the various Squire's lawns has also paid for a lot of the machinery that we have had to buy, shooting in the woods has played its part, teaching fly fishing has also helped and of course although I have not mentioned it before, we have taken in pupils who either wanted to learn the farming business or latterly one got the chap who wanted to learn how to become a Golf Club Secretary and I did not teach for free.

So can we leave the selling 'thing' till it actually becomes alive, if of course it ever does, for I am, as they say, quite happy in my work.

I should have mentioned that gallant band of *FOUNDER MEMBERS* who years ago when we first started loaned us the large sum of fifty guineas each, or was it pounds, I confess that I have forgotten, but during the last five or so years we have held a sort of 'get together', had a drink or two and got someone to draw three names out of a hat and I then paid back the gentlemen concerned what I owed them. But as far as I know we still have some five names, and their whereabouts are unknown to me.

With some reluctance I have had to put a stop to what used to be called the *Captain's Table*. Let me try and explain. The whole idea behind the original scheme was to choose a running mate for the Captain to be, but so many people were put up by various cliques, none of which were the slightest use to the Captain elect. In most cases the problem was personalities, the two men would never get on together.

So we now have *The President's Committee* and they comprise the President himself, the Present Captain, the Captain Elect, the Past Immediate Captain, The Secretary and myself. In this manner the Captain Elect will be able to choose his running mate himself, someone who he likes and who he can get on with.

I never thought that I would have to explain to grown men and women and golfing ones at that as to what exactly is meant by a five day member, but last night in the Club House, a new five day member who had been caught playing on a Sunday *with* a guest who hadn't paid his green fee, said that in his considered opinion he thought that it meant that he could play *any* five days during the seven days in the week that *he* chose. I was able to tell him gently, otherwise.

I get some silly complaints in my 'surgery' that I hold every day, bar Sundays, when I reckon I owe myself a rest, and this was from a member who came into the office and held up a pair of torn trousers, and said, "Just look at these, quite ruined." "I couldn't agree more," I said and then asked him how it happened and how in particular he thought that I was to blame.

The practice ground of about five acres runs, at its top end where we have built a small practice green, next door to another field where we keep some sheep. The sheep are moved about the remaining acres having been, if you remember, banished from the golf course, because of their uncivilized habit of sleeping in the bunkers and ejecting, throughout the night, loads of you know what. Members then, for some reason or other always persuaded their golf balls to land in this dark mass, which made their balls somewhat discoloured. The sheep were then ushered out to pastures in which there were no bunkers (and people talk about cruelty to dumb animals).

Now quite unknown to this complaining torn trousered member, you have to erect a fence so as to keep animals into a space of the farmer's choice and more often than not you make the fence with barbed wire.

So when this idiot of a member drove his ball out of the practice ground into this field with the sheep he chose to clamber over the wire concerned, quite ignoring the *two* styles that we had erected on a 200 yard fence.

So when I heard all this, instead of apologizing, I let forth on this fool action of bending and loosening my fence so that *my* sheep could get out so as to get his bloody ball. I also added for good measure that as he had reached the age of puberty, he ought to hang onto the twin *objet d'art* that the good Lord had given him.

He left without a word, holding his torn trousers in one hand and possibly his fury in the other.

CUPS AND PRIZES

I was told the other day by a member who has become bored with winning cups and was wondering as to what else might be available should he perchance win another.

I have the feeling that his wife is behind this for looking up his particular record, he has over the last nine years won some 12 cups and I think that she is fed up with polishing them. I could present him with some ghastly bit of glass ware should he win the next 'do', but his house and others are probably bulging with glass, so what else?

I then had this, for me, quite a bright idea, and when I met the wife, the other day, taking her slice in hand, I asked her whether she and of course husband would like to come along to the Cash and Carry and there fill up her basket to the tune of, say £50. The answer was "Yes, please."

And this idea became quite universal. Some members liked the odd Cup engraved for all to see how good they had been on a certain date, but the greater majority liked the concept of being trundled around our particular Cash and Carry.

RATS

These little somewhat unpleasant creatures reared their heads with the advent of a Society who we shall avoid in the future, but they started it for one of their members was 'graffiti' minded for he scribbled on one of our loo walls that we had rats by the tee on the 16th and he didn't like rats. So we went to inspect and there was a hole in the chalk with some rat droppings around it.

A phone call to the Local Government produced the 2 i/c Rodent Operator for his boss was away. He came un-announced, but he kindly left a note saying that he was no longer a Rat Catcher but a Rodent Operator and would call again when I was free.

He didn't, but his boss did by appointment, and was a bit put out when he found that he was expected to walk at least a quarter of a mile, and hadn't I a Land Rover or something similar, to which I replied that I had a tractor or three and he would be welcome to sit on the trailer. We walked.

He viewed the hole and declared that it would cost me £5 an hour for one of his work people to come out and scatter poison down the hole to which I declined his offer and said that I would insert a hose attached to the exhaust of a mower down the hole, for the same result.

Then the dustmen went on strike (I can assure you I am still on the question of the erudite scribbling on our loo walls) so I rang up the Local Council once again and asked them whether I could place my number of rubbish bags down a hole and cover it up. Very good idea they said and this is what we did, but the number one Rodent Opp. had heard through the grapevine about this somewhat novel effort of strike breaking and came out hot foot and demanded what authority I had to dig holes round the place. To which I gave him the name and for interest's sake, the rank of the man responsible for the said hole for didn't I know that I would once again get rats feeding on my rubbish. I wrote it down for him. Field Marshal Herman Goering. The hole concerned was made during the last war by a scuttling Hun wending his way back to Hunland and dropping his unused bomb.

SQUATTING

I used to have a degree of sympathy with the odd squatter that we collected over the years, but today I must admit that the patience is wearing a wee bit thin.

Take this chap, nice man in many ways, pleasant wife, but he was quite unable to get up in the morning. Day after day he would clock in at least an hour late. At first I stood it and his excuses. Under the weather, but you saw him in the pub every night. Wife was ill, but she was in the pub as well. The alarm clock didn't go off, so I gave him an old one of mine which worked perfectly.

Finally I looked him straight in the eye and said, "Tomorrow, be on time or we finish on the next pay day."

He never turned up for work at all, so I sent him a written notice, giving him a month to shift, and that was two months and a few days ago.

So I went to court and obtained an order for him and his family to leave my property in another month's time, which meant that he had been squatting for three months. One somewhat funny thing about the whole case is the electricity for his house, which in the normal way of things, I used to pay and he would then pay me, but he asked the Electricity Company to change things over from my name to his, and *now* the electricity is going to be cut off because he hasn't paid his bill, and I *know* he is going out to work, for I know the man he is working for, who asked me a while ago as to whether I had found this chap to be a good time-keeper!

Anyway, it all ended quite quietly, he left before the order was to be executed, left the place spotless and after a month or two, he wrote to me and asked me for a reference!

I did in fact write him one, I gave his good points and I also for good measure, gave his only bad one — Time.

Now I have, with countless others, adopted a quite different system. When I engage a man, I ask for a deposit, for want of a better word of some £200 which I invest for him and he can have it back as long as he abides by the letter of his contract. I inscribe it with the words *YOUR WORD IS YOUR BOND*. I have had no trouble with squatters since I adopted that ploy.

It is odd I find, where you try and write. For years have written in either a scruffy office with two or three phones yelling at me, or in our new offices where I am segregated like a leper from all and sundry, till now. I have taken this aged machine to the top of our old house and I look out onto the practice ground which I find is bliss. There is nobody to say that I am wanted on one phone after another. There are no members who are livid that either the loo paper is too hard/soft or the greens want watering as they cannot stop their pitching ball.

I can, with the aid of some powerful glasses get a free lesson from Ken Adwick, our excellent Pro, who is viewing at this moment a female some few hundred yards from me with a distinct look of boredom. She is swinging away and by the look on her face, she is happy in her work, but by the end of her lesson, I must find some grass seed as she is producing an excellent tilth.

Then there is the left hander, a male this time, who is fast getting into the swing of things and the products of his swings are landing nearer and nearer the club house windows and looking further over towards the badger set on the side of the hill, there is just the glint of brown and white fur, sunning him or herself, with its feet in the air, strange because Mr Brock the badger is more at home during the night hours than in this brilliant sunshine.

With the window open I can hear the roar of the bulldozers on the site of the old holiday camp, now defunct and I must have a word in the ear of the head driver who with a careless use of his left hand has swiped off at least 15 feet off the garden of the bungalow that we own and to add insult to injury has tipped three large tree roots over the fence into the garden.

I must not day dream and get back to golfing business for we have been inundated with applications for the post of Head Greenkeeper. Some as far away as Scotland, others almost next door and one from a famous club on which I played at the other day.

I have learnt the hard way over the years about engaging staff from far away, for they, when they apply in the first place always insist that I pay their passage, whether by train or the petrol for their car, and more often than not I have discussed this with other Secretaries and we have found that we both have paid the same man for his journey and then, as in one instance It was found that the man in question merely wanted a free visit to his girl friend who lived nearby. Now I say to the applicant, *if* you get the job I will pay your fare, otherwise no.

MY BOAT

I am getting more and more requests from members who used to come sailing with me and were, in the main as sick as two dogs, that I exchange my nice Nicholson 38 Ketch, all of 14 tons to a motor boat, or as us sailing people call them, somewhat rudely, Gin Palaces.

It was George who started all this, for he would be sick on a dampish pavement let alone in a force five or six leaning over at an angle of 25 degrees off the French coast. George found it even tricky to accept what was then a free drink leaning over at this angle and came the day when George wanted to wander off in a staggering fashion to the 'heads' and there he found it was almost impossible to find the zip, let alone undo it and he seemed to spend hours finding what he was searching for, and his aim when he at last dragged out this shrivelled half frozen *objet d'art* left a lot to be desired. No more, said George when we finally tied up back onto the pontoon at Brighton, get yourself something that says upright.

So I thought about this and came the day when I was on my own down at Brighton, patching up this and that and a man came along and asked *if* I ever wanted to sell her, would I give him a ring. I said I would, but before I got in the car to drive home, I called in at the Brokers shop and asked what was the current price for my class of boat.

With a price in mind to which I added at least 50% I rang this man up after a week or so and told him that I might just consider. But the price would have to be very good. He never hesitated, the deal was done within a week and there I was for the first time in years — boatless.

I then concentrated on finding a sea-worthy craft that would take at least half a dozen passengers, plus myself and probably a mate of mine who knew what he was doing round boats.

After a month I found what I wanted, the owner had died and the wife was not interested in boats. She did 30 knots, had twin diesel engines and was an excellent sea going craft for I took her out myself from the Medway where she was moored and wandered up the east coast in quite a big sea.

So I bought her and still had some change left out of the two deals, changed from Brighton Marina to a berth on the Medway and members flocked down to come out fishing on our 42 foot Nelson.

I never told George that it was he and his zip that had finally persuaded me, but although I missed the quiet of sailing, the Medway was an excellent base, there was always something to see.

THE LAW

Tricky thing, laws. We were caught the other day by our worthy representative of the law drinking in the bar after drinking up time and we have, or at least, I have been warned.

Members must understand that just because we are a privately owned Golf Club, this does not mean that we can do what we want and drink all the hours that God gave us. We are allowed to consume drink for nine and a half hours per day and a bit less on Sunday.

But, and it is a big but, if you the Member held the licence then although the nine and a half hours would remain the same, you could alter your times of drinking. For you would be a registered club, always of course, the Bench allowed. You would then be able to take part in the fascinating game of VAT; you would then be able to pay all the bills for *your* drink at the right time; you could, seeing that it would be *your* Club House, leased of course from the Company on a yearly tenancy, get in the habit of paying the rates, the electricity bill, not forgetting the small item of wages for the bar staff and the cook house, unless of course you thought you could 'do' the bar yourselves on some sort of roster system and maybe the cook house as well.

And then think what you would do with all the profits. The mind boggles.

I sent all that to your Chairman of the General Committee and his reply was interesting but I regret unprintable, so it would appear that you will have to continue to put up with me.

I was asked the other day by a member as to whether we would service his mower for him? More than willing to do the 'blade' part of the business but not the engine. So wheel it in when you want.

I am told by my Members that if my weekly news sheet is *not* where it should be on a Saturday, the complaints book will overflow, but in this case, and I do know that I have been AWOL for at least a couple of weeks, but I have been watching my Mother die.

Firstly week by week and then day by day and finally hour upon ghastly hour and the worst part was that she knew she was going, months ago and she kept on apologizing to me, her only son, that she would not be there to advise and assist, if I had a problem, but she said that she had to choose (as if she had a choice) between staying with me or going off to join my Father, and those two were really a love match.

So I am now alone and we cremated her and scattered her ashes where she asked and I put up a little head stone which, because she was a keen gardener, read:

> The kiss of the sun for pardon,
> The song of the birds for mirth,
> One is nearer God's heart in a garden,
> Than anywhere else on earth.

Sorry about all that personal stuff but I wrote it, really to see whether I could.

Rumours. The fickle 'jades' they are, the present or current issue is that the Secretary is leaving, the subs are going up by 25% and I have sold the place to an Oil Baron. He isn't, they are not, and I haven't, but on the subs angle, they will be going up at around about 18%, clubs around us are going up from 25% to 50%, take your pick.

But I am 65 years young and I have not as yet thought as to how long I want to continue in this particular rat race, these thoughts were prompted by a ring on my front door and there was a man, shielding of all things, a vast Rolls who enquired as to whether I was who I was, so to speak and then, without a pause asked me whether it was true that this place was for sale?

I replied that I wanted to finish my lunch first before giving him a straight answer, got his name and phone number, said good morning and that was that, but it gave me food for thought and nothing more, I hasten to add.

Sad news for me in particular and you in general, for today my very good friend and excellent Secretary, Adrian Boler, decided that enough was enough and he wanted a well earned rest with effect from December 10th of this year, 1982.

So I have yet once again to look for someone to fill Adrian's place, an impossible job as far as I was concerned, for he and I were never under the impression that one employed the other, we were friends and those special people from a man's point of view, one can count generally on one hand. Acquaintances, yes, hundreds of them, but friends — that was another matter.

To find someone who is an expert in every facet of this mini estate, is not easy when you come to think about it. He, or for that matter, she should be able to talk about subjects far divorced from golf, such as rearing game birds which we did in our woods; know the difference between meadow grass and agrostic bent; be able to mow the semi rough in a couple of hours; take a soil sample and find out its pH value, between helping out in the bar and tossing a steak into a pan. In short everything from the womb to the tomb if that be the right phrase.

My thanks to those kind members who let me through this morning, for I was cutting the rough at a fast 4 m.p.h and time was of the essence, although the actions of another member might be worth recording for I was approaching the tee on the 14th and was about to turn on the headland when I noticed a golfer on the tee, place his ball on the peg, never looked anywhere as far as my anxious gaze could see and we were only some 20 yards apart and he drove. The ball missed me by a whisker to which I was pleased about but felt that I really could spare the time to have a short, possibly sharp chat with this 'couldn't care less golfer'. So cut the engine and invited this man to sit in my seat, I made it plain that I would clean the seat first. And let me borrow one of his clubs and of course a ball and then tell me his thoughts *after* I had struck another ball in his general direction.

I didn't get the chance to carry out this pleasant exercise for his answer which really should go down in golfing history, was — and he said it with a smile too — that he thought the glass some 20″ away from my face was shatter proof!

My apologies to those of you who were slightly put out by the security check that went on last Monday, starting at about 08.00 to

12.00. Some explanations are due to soothe your ruffled feathers.

We do this once or sometimes twice a year and quite often we find a player who has not paid his sub for the year and of course has not paid a green fee (what a thought) and this is slightly naughty.

Even worse we find a player with this year's disc on his bag which *should* denote that he *had* paid his sub, only to find that the disc concerned belongs to someone else who *has* paid but somebody pinched his disc. That is *very* naughty, and to then find that he is *not* a member here or anywhere else for that matter, gives me the feeling that I would like to march the wretched man along to the nearest 'nick'. But life is too short and besides I have not that sort of time.

VOUCHERS

Someone asked me the other day whether we handed out vouchers to a member who introduced a seven day member. The answer is yes, you receive £20 worth of vouchers and likewise £10 for a five day member, always assuming that the person concerned is accepted.

But the other day a member who had better remain anonymous asked for an appointment to introduce a friend of his.

This so-called friend slouched into the Secretary's office, didn't bother to knock, sat himself down in a chair and listened with some interest to the phone conversation that the Secretary was having. He had not shaved for a week, a bath had not had the undoubted pleasure of viewing his sweating torso for sometime, be was dressed, (if that is the right description) in a sweat shirt which was filthy and he was smoking the stub of a foul smelling cigar. His sponsor was told that he would not receive any vouchers.

MUCKING ABOUT IN BOATS

I was asked the other day whether I would take out two couples, all members, who would like to 'slip' at about 17.00 on a Friday and return to tie up on the Sunday evening, and could they fish and also would it be possible to go ashore to a pub on Saturday evening.

This meant a two day passage give or take an hour or so and both couples wanted to be free of any cooking which meant that I would have to engage someone to do that chore and also they wanted a price to cover the lot, i.e., food and drink.

So asked for and got, £150 per couple.

Then we had the slight snag as to which cabin each couple would have. On the Nelson the forward cabin had its own head and basin whereas the aft cabin only had a basin and that meant that the owners would have to come through the centre cabin where I and the cook slept.

So they tossed up for it which saved a lot of trouble.

I was lucky enough to obtain the services of a nice chap who *was* a cook at a pub and who had a week's holiday and was keen on boats, so together we went down to the cash and carry and bought enough food and drink for the two days and took it all down to the boat that Friday afternoon and stowed it before the passengers arrived at about 17.00 hrs.

Before we got the mooring ropes fore and aft in board and stowed away I told my four passengers and one crew, the rule of the sea in general and this little craft in particular. Firstly that if they wanted to go on deck they *had* to wear a life jacket and I gave them one each and made certain that they knew how it worked, then came the tricky bit because as I have said before I did in fact insist on a real-life overboard drill and I called for volunteers. Nobody was all that keen and so the passengers drew lots and one of the men got the short straw so to speak. I made certain that he could swim and told him when and where I wanted him to pretend to fall into the drink.

I also told the others what they had to do and in the end they all became quite interested and keen to see what actually happened.

And so in a quiet spot in the Medway, I tipped the wink to our intrepid 'man overboard' and over he went with a shout of 'HELP'.

Slight panic occurred especially with the wife of the man in the 'drink', for in her haste she all but clouted him over the head with our long boat hook, but eventually a laughing 'passenger' was hauled aboard and to celebrate the happy event a tot of rum was issued all round.

We arrived off the Isle of Sheppy about midday and my passengers wanted to fish, which was fine and I chose a spot out of the way of passing traffic and asked for some assistance in dropping the 'hook'.

One wife enquired as to why we could not tie up on those two 'sticks' which were visible on our port quarter. I explained that those two 'sticks', as she called them, were the twin masts of a ship called the *Montgomery* which was sunk by some wandering U-boat during the war and she had gone down with an alleged five hundred tons of TNT on board which so far had not gone up.

My crew or passenger requested that we shift to safer ground forthwith and we went down the Swale and anchored off that nice pub on the port side whose name escapes me and there we fished with some success till the evening when I had to transport four passengers across some two hundred yards of quite choppy water to the pub of their choice in our rubber dinghy.

I might say that we all had a somewhat damp supper, but returned in the same fashion, getting wetter by the yard, but we all had other dry clothes and a happy evening was had by all.

We were fortunate in that coming back up the Medway to our berth we followed the hordes of small boats that were escorting the *Endurance* from the Falklands war up to her berth.

SALE RUMOURS

Yes I must come clean. I have had an offer from a couple of people, but as I said years ago, if and when we sell I must in duty bound offer it to the Members first. So I am offering you, the Member, in a formal fashion the chance to buy the Golf Course, including the Club House, the Locker Room complex, the Office Block, the Machine Shed, which might as well be called Lot 1, for the sum of £350,000 subject to contract. I sent this to your Captain and asked for a reply by December 9th 1982. The ball, gentlemen is in your court.

You must understand that the three tied cottages and the manor house, plus the practice ground, together with the remaining 100 acres is not included in this offer.

The tools and equipment are subject to valuation should you wish to purchase them.

I understand that you did in fact hold a meeting and that you came up with a figure of £20,000. I am not clear what this entails, but I feel that if this is your best offer for the above property, then

I must with some reluctance, turn you down and look elsewhere.

There are at the moment some three fairly serious buyers who wander around the place from morning to night and the other day I had two of the families concerned in my office to answer some of their countless hundreds of questions. Such as, who tells the ground staff what to do? Answer, you do. Who orders the drink? — you do. Who runs the office? — you do. Who looks after the woods? — you do. What about the other 100 acres or so, who looks after that? — you do.

And so on and so forth, and this went on for about an hour without anyone repeating a single thing. Phew, they both said.

LOCKER ROOMS

Years ago, if you remember we had a time clock on the locker rooms which opened the door at a certain time and shut it at night. One of our more charming members forgot this and just *had* to get in to get something, so broke the lock, this was about a month ago. Nothing daunted we went and bought another time clock because this is what your Committee wanted and who was I to argue (i merely pay the bills). Now once again some dear chap has bust the lock *and* the door, or most of it and this time we shall do what other clubs do which is to shut the place at a certain time at night and open it at a certain time in the morning.

You will just have to remember that *if* you are playing in Glasgow at crack of dawn tomorrow, then you must take your clubs and clothes with you. I get slightly fed up when the back door rings in the middle of supper and there is a member with a Dobermann hanging onto him, saying that he left his wallet behind and please come and open up for him.

A lot of my time now is spent, or wasted quite often by would be buyers coming to the house and asking whether they can buy *one* cottage, to which I always say no. Then others come along and want to buy *just* the Manor House and again I say *no* because I now have two people who want the whole 'shebang' which is a much simpler solution and I think we have found a buyer who will take over the course and everything bar the house and the other 100 or so acres in May/June, but will keep my fingers crossed till contracts are signed.

121

But in the meantime, sale or no sale, life must go on and golf work in the shape of keeping this place in a satisfactory state so as to hand over to the new owners is of paramount importance.

I mentioned that Golf Club Secretaries in the south of England do meet, generally once a year and have a game of golf and there is a guest speaker and I had sleepless nights because I and one other owner of a golf club were asked to tell the rest of the members present the main difference between a members' club and one that is privately owned. We were the guest speakers. It ruined my day, especially as we tossed up, this other owner and I, and of course I lost and decided that I had better 'bat' first.

So I started off with the knotty problem as to why golf clubs in general never make any money, or very little out of either the catering side or the drink side in a club house.

My way, I said, was to charge each member the sum of £50 on top of his annual sub and this gave him a voucher book, containing 50 one pound vouchers, so that the member concerned merely bought his food and drink by handing over sufficient vouchers to cover the amount concerned. I pointed out also that he could not buy a box of matches for 5p and get cash in change.

So as we have some 700 members, that generates an immediate £35,000 which, as we make a profit of about 50% on what we sell, that £35,000 comes down to £17,500. Add to this last figure some 50 'boot' members who never, under any circumstance, dream of being seen dead in the club house, this brings the last figure back to £20,000.

Then there is the one armed bandit which, when it paid out a paltry £25, was hardly ever patronized. Now we have a machine that, for the large sum of 10p you *might* win yourself £200. Queues form on a week end to play the thing, so much so that at times during the summer, we have had to put up so-called starting sheets giving each member 10 minutes of play. The profit was considerable.

Also about the club house, you must train your staff and the prettier they are, the better, to make the member feel that the girl has been waiting for hours for him to turn up. It is not the slightest use for the girl to pull a pint and then retire to a corner and file her nails.

Then you should pay your club house staff a small percentage of the net profit, and you want to do this at Christmas.

You want a couple of decent snooker tables and the playing concerned is controlled by a light meter which should work out at about 50p per game or more.

If you have woods on your course, go in for wood burning stoves, both for heating and hot water, and if you have tied cottages, then install the same stoves, but smaller and give your work people free wood as long as they cut enough for the club house in their own time.

Other money making schemes involves the *Golfing Ladder* which brings in a lot of money. This is the same as the old squash ladder where you challenge and play the name above you on the board. You give him 50p and you give the club 50p and at the end of the year, generally on Christmas Day, I give the man on top of the 'heap' £300, in vouchers, of course.

Most of you, when you mow your greens throw your clippings away, you do the same with the cores out of a green. I mix the lot together, put them through a shredder and sell a ½ cwt bag for sufficient to raise some £3,000 per year.

Still on mowing, you mow your greens generally in the summer five days a week, use the other two days to mow big lawns in your area, give your man who does the mowing a percentage and that generally is worth another £2,000 per year.

GUNS

As long as you have some game about, this is worth about 1,000 guineas per gun per year.

The next is a bit unfair for I own an ocean going yacht and members pay quite large sums to come out for a day and either fish or, as I have passed my navigating exams, I teach them something about that particular, pleasant pastime.

I am a dowser and members want to learn something about this so called skill, so I teach them. I teach them how to cast a fly, but like the Golf Pro., I charge for my lessons.

Then there are young pupils who want to learn farming, so I teach them. There are people who want to learn something about becoming a golf club Secretary, again I pass on what I have learned over the last 16 years, but repeating myself, all this brings in money.

There are couples who want to go into the pub trade. Teach them how to pull a pint, clean a pipe, do the books, the examples are legion. But the main difference between you, the members' club and myself is I do *not* have to ask some vast committee as to whether you will be *allowed* to do any of these things that I have just explained to you, I just get on with it.

I then sat down and listened with great interest to my other owner of a golf course and he had one or two 'wrinkles' that I must have a think about, and when afterwards, we got a chance to chat together, he, I gather, is going to try out some of my money making schemes.

Selling a place like this with all its different little bits takes a considerable time, not helped one little bit by the would-be buyer's solicitors who wanted every but and bolt listed and in triplicate.

It is not enough to say that here is a tractor manufactured by Mr Ferguson. They want the year it was made, all its numbers, chassis and otherwise and bearing in mind that I had been on the place for some 27 years and am a hoarder by nature if not by inclination, it was a vast task and I rebelled.

I got my tape recorder, the one with which in the early days, I used to natter into whilst having my breakfast after delivering 1,000 pints of milk and I laid out *all* the hoarded so-called wealth of 27 years and I went from one object to the next and I taped the lot and sent the tape to the solicitors.

To be honest, they were not all that keen on the idea, but I told them that was what I was prepared to do, take it or leave it, *or* should they wish to come down and view the laid out treasures, they were most welcome.

Then you have the rates and where I have paid to and when the new chap starts, the Electricity, the water, etc., and at last, but not of course least, we have you, for if perchance you paid your 'unjust' dues, say a mere month ago, then I have to work out that $1/_{12}$th of what you have kindly paid and the new man has the remainder. Not forgetting for a moment that you have paid VAT which also has to come off.

We shall be going off for our usual fortnight to the same spot in Brittany and in fact the same house that we rented last year, leaving the place in the sure hands of Peter Sauberg who took over from Adrian Boler a few months ago, with the thought that in a month or two you will be rid of me and furniture vans will be wending their way down our narrow lanes to our new house.

Time passes. Only a week but I have bad news for you in that in the middle of our rest cure, my able Secretary rang up to say that the whole deal was off with a capital O. The new man had changed his mind and now if I wanted to proceed with the selling, then I had better put the whole thing into the hands of an agent, which I did after trundling back from sunny France.

The agents were Humberts and they got hold of me a fortnight after we were told that the deal was off to say that it was now on again. Nothing to do with me, but it would seem to have been a great waste of the new owner's money for to deal through an agent costs a great deal more than dealing with the person from whom you buy something, i.e., me. Still that is his affair and nothing to do with me, but once again to put the members in the picture, I am selling the golf course and everything on the 1st August and vacating the house on the 16th August and departing with the aid of Pickfords to Sussex to our new home by the sea.

At 12.00 hrs on July 18th 1983, Adrian Boler, my ex-Secretary, was released from the filthy thing that had him by the throat and went to the land where there are no handicaps of any kind. We who were close to him breathed a sigh of relief for the last few days have been a great strain as of course he was under constant drugs so as to ease the pain.

Thirteen more days to go and the end of an era in our lives lasting some 27 years when we arrived in Woodlands with twelve hens and three heifers, two small children and loaded down with a large fat mortgage.

The hens are long since gone, but their progeny abound to the delight of nearby foxes. The heifers became cows and bred well and we carted their produce amounting to some 1,000 pints per day around our immediate area of 28 miles.

The children grew up and they married and gave us seven

grandchildren, the mortgage departed and were free to make our own mistakes which we did with monotonous regularity till this day. And ever week, more or less without fail, I produced a so-called News Sheet of about 1,000 words, sometimes more if there was something interesting to relate as to who had done whom, where and when and possibly how. If I did not then the complaints book, which I read with great interest every week, asked where is this week's News Sheet.

So where does one start the ending of some 800,000 words, ill-written in the main with lousy spelling but with, I assure you, the best intentions.

To me the answer is quite clear. I must start with the members both past and present who have put up with my puny efforts to produce a golf course. They have taken my mistakes and there have been many, with generally a kind heart and with the thought that the silly 'B' won't do that one again.

And from the Members to the Presidents both past and present who have done us proud in more ways than one and to the last one in my time anyway, who I have had the pleasure of knowing for many a long year, he enters into the many games of golf that he feels he ought to and never makes the mistake of winning anything and has the nice habit of presenting the owner of this golf course with a ball or three, always of course wrapped. And lastly we share, he and I, a liking for Malt.

And to the four Secretaries that I was fortunate to know in the sixteen years that I owned this Golf Club, ending with Peter Saubergue who was the only one who had any experience of sitting on a tractor and learning everything pertaining to the efficient running of a golf course.

And to all the other staff, both past and present, who have looked after the course, I wish you well and even the ones who couldn't for some quirk of their nature avoid hitting anything solid in the 200 acres that we have, more or less, of golf course, I am sure that you didn't mean it, but between these four walls and for your ears only — You were bloody costly while you lasted.

Even to those who gently squatted with us for months on end, who stole from us with monotonous regularity, I hope you find a better squat and that the pickings are easier as you both grow older.

To our present staff in the Club House who do such an excellent job and put up with all the idiosyncrasies of the members, and last but not least to the Professional shop ably led by Ken Adwick. To all of you thank you for your kindness over the last sixteen years.

And now the time has come as the Bishop is alleged to have said to the actress, that we must be up and about. Pickfords are waiting, all four vans are outside in the drive, packed to the brim with 83 tea chests, representing all that we have gathered together in our 42 years of married life.

All the furniture has different coloured stickers on them and all that Pickfords have to do when they reach our new house by the sea is to match up the colours to the same colours on the doors of the rooms. What could go wrong?

Needless to say it did, my wife, bless her, is a creature of habit, and when she has finished driving her Mini round Kent, she always, without fail, puts her car keys in a particular kitchen drawer.

Pickfords when they started were given instructions to empty everything. This they did and, of course, the four vans started off and were soon out of sight. We got into our two cars to follow.

I could, because I always keep my car keys on me, but the keys of the Mini were at that moment speeding down to sunny Sussex.

This necessitated a furious placing of wires here and there in the Mini so that we could get her started and what is more, catch up with Pickfords, for we had to be at the new house before them as we had the keys. We did it, the pair of us, but only just.

So here we are in the autumn of our lives, in a nice house, maybe its a bit big, but old habits die hard for we had been living in a big house with seven bedrooms, four loos, and cellars, stretching for yards for twenty-seven years.

Nobody can build in front of us for the sea comes up to the garden wall and behind us is the golf course where the powers that be there, have kindly consented to allow me to become a member.

Slight snag now arises for in more or less my first game at my new club, two faces appear, who were old members of mine yesteryear on my own course and they buttonholed me to do something about some problem that was worrying them and others concerning the way this club is run.

I was told by these two that we never had this problem in *your* club — do something. So I told them that I was a new member here and I would not dream of offering advice on anything unless I was asked to do so. The way that this club was run was nothing to do with me, I merely paid my sub, enjoyed my golf and the friends that I had made and I wanted peace in the autumn of my life, but it does raise an interesting point or points.

Who as a matter of interest is in charge of the modern golf club? Who tells who what to do?

Is it the Chairman, the President, the current Captain or perhaps the Secretary or maybe (but God forbid) a majority vote of the Club Committee? And one must not forget the Head Green-Keeper. He, at least, should have a first rate knowledge of actually working the course side of the club. But supposing that the Head Green-Keeper is not really up to scratch, then who tells *him* what he should be doing?

And turning that last sentence round a trifle, who does the Head Green-Keeper ask when *he* knows he wants a certain article of machinery. Take for instance that his trailer gangs are worn out and he wants the Club to invest in a *mounted* seven mower attachment that is controlled by the PTO (Power Take Off) and the hydraulic lifting power of the tractor concerned. Who, out of the above hierarchy has the slightest knowledge of what he is talking about?

In my humble opinion the overall power of any Golf Club, whether it be an Owners' Club, a Members' Club or even a Club run by the RDC should be in the hands of the Secretary.

But the Secretary concerned *must* have a working knowledge of everything that moves on his 'domain' and of course he should liaise with somebody in the Club, whether it be the Chairman or who. But he should *not* be dictated to by some worthy committee man whether he be a peer or a plumber.

The ground staff should not number more than three, always providing that they have the right tools and they *must* be able to play golf and matches *must* be arranged with other Green-Keepers of other Clubs and the Home Club must pay for the costs of that particular match.

The Club House. The knotty problem of making it pay, to my mind always comes back to the voucher system where you charge the member, say £100 on top of his annual sub and you present him with a voucher book containing 100 £1 vouchers and then make certain that *your* prices are at least 2½% lower than anyone else in the immediate area.

But the main problem about a golf Club House is that the members want one but they are not prepared to support one to the same extent that they probably support their village pub, thus making them support it with the voucher scheme. Golf Club prizes might also be given in vouchers.

Now, if you don't mind you two old members, I want to get on with my game. See you in the 19th sometime.